Leave Nothing to Chance

15 Principles for Success and the Stories that Inspired Them

Foster Owusu & John Solleder

as told to Mona Andrei

Foreword by
Larry Thompson

Leave Nothing to Chance: 15 Principles for Success and
the Stories that Inspired Them

Copyright © 2020 by Foster Owusu & John Solleder

Published by:
Tremendous Leadership
P.O. Box 267
Boiling Springs, PA 17007
717-701-8159   800-233-2665
www.TremendousLeadership.com

This book or parts thereof may not be reproduced in any form, stored in a retrieval system, or transmitted in any form by any means electronic, mechanical, photocopy, recording, or otherwise without prior written permission of the publisher, except as provided by United States of America copyright law and except by a reviewer who may quote brief passages in a review. All Rights Reserved.

ISBN Hardcover 978-1-949033-38-0
ISBN Paperback 978-1-949033-39-7
ISBN E-book 978-1-949033-40-3
Printed in the United States of America

Dedication

This book is dedicated to all the network marketing pioneers that have come before us. Your courage and commitment to this industry helped to break down walls and stigmas. Thanks to you, people around the world continue to better their lives simply by doing what they love. As this industry continues to grow, it is our hope that individuals will continue to build their businesses on a foundation of integrity, respect, and genuine compassion for others.

Contents

Foreword by Larry Thompson vii

The "Why" Behind this Book ix

1   Principle 1: Wake Up Excited for the Day—An Art and a Practice..1

2   Principle 2: Listen to YOUR Reason—It's the Heart of the Matter..15

3   Principle 3: Instill the Right Mindset—And You'll Have no Choice but to Succeed............................27

4   Principle 4: Create Balance—It's the Key to Staying on Track..37

5   Principle 5: Commit. Or Risk Giving up too Soon.........45

6   Principle 6: Look Back on Life—There's no Time Like Now to Learn from Your Past 55

7   Principle 7: Observe the Financial Domino Effect.........67

8   Principle 8: Watering the Seed 75

9   Principle 9: Showing Love for Others 85

10   Principle 10: Train yourself to Think the Way that Successful People Think..............................93

11	Principle 11: Build a Better Future—Starting Today	101
12	Principle 12: Lead with Integrity	109
13	Principle 13: Success Doesn't Just Happen. Success Happens Just.	117
14	Principle 14: Imagine that this is Your Last Chance	125
15	Principle 15: Get Ready for Your Next Level	133
16	And Now It's Up to You!	141
17	Meet the Many Faces of Our Industry	143
Recommended Reading		219

Foreword by Larry Thompson

I have been involved in the network marketing world for over 53 years and have mentored thousands of individuals who have gone on to become leaders. These are leaders that today, I'm proud to call my friends. Two such people are John Solleder and Foster Owusu. I first met John in Hartford, Connecticut, back in 1983. At the time, he was a young man just starting out. He had no money and drove around in a broken-down US mail truck. Yet he had tons of potential. I saw his drive right away. His willingness to work hard and his leadership skills got my attention. Even after he left the company that I was consulting for at the time, we kept in touch and I watched him become one of the top earners at a water filter company during the mid-1980s. From there, I watched as he followed the same pattern of becoming a top earner at a diet cookie company a few years later as he took this company around the world.

I selected him as one of my twelve inner-circle members for Wealth-Building and again watched his leadership in action as he brought hundreds of people to my training classes. I then helped him put on the corporate hat and worked with him to guide another friend's company with strategies that grew very rapidly and continued even after he came to the realization that the corporate world wasn't for him.

From there, he went back to his calling in the network marketing industry and, of course, continues to excel to this day as he helps lead his current company, where he has been for over 24 years now. He has always been a great student and teacher in his own right. I have watched him through multiple companies and situations where he always chooses to do the right thing to help himself, his teams, and several companies to "get it right."

Through John, I met Foster Owusu and was immediately taken by Foster's smile and life story of not letting poverty as a youth in Ghana deter him from creating a better life for himself and his family in Canada. Foster also attended my trainings and always asked great questions. His approach to leadership in his current company has been unique in that he has been the first in many categories, and he continues to lead today. We both share great admiration for the Amway founders and Foster had a unique relationship early in his career with Rich DeVos.

These two men—John and Foster—have walked the walk and talked the talk, and I'm proud to say that they are both dear friends of mine as they continue to help and guide others with integrity and the very principles they live by and share in this book.

Larry Thompson

The "Why" Behind this Book

If you know us in person, you know that we are all about calling a spade *a spade*. Both our businesses and our relationships are built on our capacity to be straightforward, vulnerable, and supportive of our networks. It's what we expect from ourselves. It's what we expect from each other. It's also what we *give* of ourselves. The way we see it, these three combined characteristics—being straightforward, vulnerable, and supportive—are the mother of sincerity. Sincerity leads to trust, and trust is the foundation for building long-term relationships with people that you resonate with. And "people" are exactly what our businesses and our successes are based on.

While we're both in the network marketing industry, a business model that is based on genuine relationships and personal self-development, the principles in this book can be applied to any business model, whether you're leading a company or are a member of a team. We wrote this book because we believe that you're just like us in that you want control over your time, your finances, and your life.

More time to spend doing the things you love, including sharing those pivotal moments in your children's lives—that school play, hockey game, or choir performance.

More control over how much money you make so that you can afford the pleasures in life, whether they be the simple ones or luxuries.

More freedom to follow your dreams and make a difference in the world.

Regardless of how you define the details of leading a "successful life," we're confident that your underlying goal is to own your time so that you can pursue your goals and focus on the things that make you happy; happiness being the ultimate goal for us all.

How do we know this? Over the years we've had the pleasure of working with thousands of people. Whether their vision of success included sitting behind a desk in a corner office or being able to take an extra vacation every year, control and freedom always played a big part in an individual's definition of leading a successful life.

In essence, you too want more from life. We're here to tell you that there's absolutely nothing wrong with that. In fact, we're here to cheer you on because (as we've discovered) the more you get from life, the more you have to give back. And by giving back, we mean contributing to the enhancement of all humanity. So even though your goals may "feel" selfish, they're really not. They're just a means to an end. Isn't that an awesome concept? It's like a win-win agreement with life itself!

And yet for many, success remains but a dream. Something that we watch others attain. Something that's too risky for us and our life situation. It's unfortunate, but the great majority of people stifle their own potential. Why? Because they feel that the nine-to-five grind offers a predictable safety net and sense of security. Yet this sense of security comes at a very high price. The cost is not only a lost sense of fulfillment where you're truly in charge of the one and only life you get to design, but a sense of deprivation as well. Depriving yourself, yes. But also depriving the world of your unique talents that can only be offered from your true self. Even if we don't know you personally, our guess is that you already know this. That's why you're reading this book. You know what you want, you just aren't sure how to get there. We can help. But before we introduce ourselves, there's one thing we'd like to make very clear:

We do not believe in get-rich-quick schemes.

We hold firm to the fact that most get-rich-quick schemes (if not all) are devised and promoted by unethical people. What happens when someone like you buys into a quick and dirty promise to riches? In the end, the only winner is the person who convinced you that you should tag along for the ride. Then what happens? We'll tell you: you're left disappointed and cheated of your time, your money, and even your dreams and aspirations.

Words to live by: If an "opportunity" seems too good to be true, it most definitely is. And don't let anyone trick you into believing otherwise!

Gaining control over your time, your finances, and your life … what does that mean exactly? Simply put, it's about doing the things that you love. Sharing your talents and passions. Living with a sense of purpose. These statements are all well-defined sentiments of success, and their attainment is a slow and steady process. One that takes work and commitment. One that is so worth the effort.

We invite you to consider the following mantra:

Anything worthwhile takes work.

Effort = Results = A Successful Life

And while most people cringe at the concept of "work" (not because they're lazy but because it's human nature to gravitate towards the easy path, the path of least resistance), it's important to note that *work* doesn't have to be hard. Or, said another way, work doesn't have to be *unappealing*.

This is especially true when the word "work" is defined by the act of doing something you love—just as we have been doing for a combined 60 years.

Not to boast but looking back and comparing the early years of our careers with today, we've even managed to impress ourselves. This is what we want for you. We want you to be able to look back over the years of your life and say, *"Wow! I did it. Look at the life I've designed!"*

And here's a great truth. One we've seen time and time again, and we think you'll find comfort in it:

You can never be too young or too old to follow your dreams. Why? Because happiness and a sense of fulfillment are ageless! At the end of this book we're also happy to share with you insights and experiences from other leaders in the industry. People that we are honored to call our colleagues and friends.

So, who are we to want such greatness for you?

We are John Solleder and Foster Owusu. Two individuals from different backgrounds and cultures with a shared vision, shared definition of success, and shared passion for helping others achieve *their* definition of success. In fact, that last one—"helping others achieve *their* definition of success"—is something we excel at. Why? Because it fits into something else that we share: good values and a strong sense of integrity.

That's right. We care. And to be frank, we couldn't have achieved the levels of success that we've attained if we didn't.

If you look at our track record, we're confident you'll agree: the reason we're good at what we do is because the principles we follow

The "Why" Behind this Book

(the ones outlined in this book) work! And not only for us, but for the people we have the honor of working with—every single day.

We may not have had the pleasure of meeting you in person (yet), so let's begin by telling you the story of how we met each other.

John's Perspective

I remember my first real meeting with Foster. There were two things that struck me right away. And if you know him, you'll know exactly what I'm talking about.

The first thing was his smile. Foster has a way of connecting with people that lets you know right away exactly how genuine he is. He listens with both of his ears, and when he smiles, you know that that smile comes from his core. Foster is one of the sincerest people I've ever had the pleasure of working with. And after all these years, I'm still proud to call him my friend.

The second thing I noticed was the way that he not only has a list of priorities, but he lives by them. First and foremost, Foster has his spiritual beliefs. His beautiful family comes in a close second. And then there's his business. Yet the three are harmonized through his commitment, dedication, and authenticity.

Watching him ... listening to him speak that first day we met ... I could see right away how clear he was on what was truly important to him, and I immediately recognized Foster as someone I wanted on my team. I knew from the moment I heard him speak that he was someone I could count on to work together as we climbed the mountain towards our business goals.

Friendships like that don't happen every day, and I can honestly say that I feel blessed to have the opportunity of knowing and working with him over these many years. He's a great field general for his team, and I'm proud to have him in my life.

That said, after he and I both authored our own books individually, I realized that it was time for us to collaborate and do something special. Something that would help other people just like us—people who want something better for themselves, their families, and their communities.

Foster's Perspective

Perhaps the best place to begin this historic journey of how John and I met is to point out that almost all auto body shop workers meet people by accident. Not in our case. I honestly believe that our paths crossed for a reason and with a purpose.

My first encounter with John was in the early 1990s. Although there wasn't a direct relationship between the two of us at the time, his name stood out in every business presentation that I attended. Even back then—close to 30 years ago—John was recognized as a leader.

Today I can honestly say that John is the pillar behind my decision to join the company that I've been with since 1999. To this day, it is partly due to my confidence in him and his capacity as a leader that I've been able to stay true to building my own organization.

When did I actually get to meet John for the very first time? The exact date was February 20, 1999. I remember it well. He was a guest speaker at a major event in Toronto, Canada, and his message, his sense of conviction and commitment … it all resonated with me. And still does to this day.

George Washington is known to have said, *"Truth will ultimately prevail where pains is taken to bring it to light."*

Anyone in business, anyone following a dream or trying to achieve a goal knows that the path to attainment is filled with moments of pain. There's commitment. A state of being that requires our constant focus. There are sacrifices. Sometimes life would just be easier if we didn't have this burning desire within us.

To this day, John's conviction and commitment resonate with my own values and sense of integrity. That foundation alone describes our long-lasting friendship, and I'm proud to call John my friend.

Leave nothing to chance. What does that mean exactly?

Regardless of what you may have been taught or led to believe, success isn't just for the chosen few. And to demonstrate this, it's time to put the cheerleading pom-poms away and formally introduce ourselves. As mentioned, we are John Solleder and Foster Owusu. Just a couple of guys with a vision, a genuine passion for helping others, and some proven principles for achieving success. Our goal with this book is to share these principles with you!

As mentioned, we've each written a book about our experiences in attaining success through our respective network marketing organizations. John's book is *Moving Up: Real-Life Secrets for Getting From Here to There,* and Foster's book is entitled *How to Fire Your Boss and Hire Yourself.*

With a shared passion for helping others to achieve their dreams, our intention for this book—the one you're now holding in your hands—is designed to help as many people as we possibly can.

While our business model happens to be network marketing (perfect grounds for helping others and seeing true value and results from our work), our process, approach, and the principles described in the following pages will pave the way to your success, no matter what industry you're in and what your goals are.

From freelancers and contract workers to entrepreneurs wanting to build their own empire. From single mothers working at balancing their many tasks, to dual income families trying to find balance. We firmly believe that the principles outlined in this book can guide anyone to a life filled with freedom, passion, purpose, and fulfillment. This is because a life of quality only happens by design.

YOUR life, YOUR design.

As the principles throughout this book reveal, success isn't a secret formula privy to only certain lucky individuals. Control over your time, finances, and life is a mindset that anyone can achieve. Sometimes all it takes is a little guidance. This book IS that guidance.

Building a business. Walking away from renting out your time so that someone else can benefit from your talents. Owning your life with a sense of purpose. Providing for your children, and even more importantly, being there when they need you. Single moms, working parents, entrepreneurs ... This book will not only provide you with the tools and insights to make your dreams for success come true but will also remind you of the importance of living a life of purpose; for yourself, for your family, and for society.

"For society?" You ask.

Yes, for society. Another strong belief that we share is that our time here on earth is about contribution. And no one can contribute wholeheartedly unless they've discovered their best self. After all, isn't that the true meaning of leading a successful life? It's simple logic: The happier you are, the more fulfilled and satisfied you are and the more you have to give:

To your kids.

To your significant other.

The "Why" Behind this Book

To your parents.

To your siblings.

To the elderly lady you take a moment to help as she struggles with her bag of groceries.

There are all kinds of business models out there. Traditional. Franchise. Product- and service-oriented. Finding fulfillment, purpose, and passion is an individual journey. We just happen to have found our happy place with network marketing.

One of the aspects of network marketing that appeals to us is that it's the only business model that fosters a built-in support system. In fact, no other business model encourages self-development and growth like network marketing. We can attribute our success to this fact.

This is important since any goal in life, whether it be building a business or developing a set of skills, faces a huge obstacle. You may know of it. This universal obstacle is maintaining focus and commitment to a goal. This obstacle goes by a few names that you may already be familiar with, procrastination and distractions being the most common. (And here you thought it was only you!)

As we've discovered throughout our many years in this industry, network marketing can be summed up by the words of author, salesperson, and motivational speaker Zig Ziglar:

> "You will get all you want in life if you help enough other people get what they want."

This is how we run our respective businesses every single day. And while we spend much of our time sharing our insights through public speaking engagements, one-on-one mentoring, and group training programs designed to help others to achieve their financial and entrepreneurial goals, our wish with this book is twofold:

1. To help as many people as possible achieve their goals.
2. To provide tangible guidelines and an easy reference for anyone who endeavors to help others.

While you may be holding this book in your hands today as a way for us to help you achieve your goals, it is more than probable that one day you'll be using the very principles outlined in this book to help others achieve their personal dreams.

Imagine your accomplishments when you will have reached a point in your life when you want to give back and help someone else achieve their dream for success!

When you build a network marketing business, your primary asset is yourself. YOU are the backbone of your business. Which is why the effort of continually investing in YOURSELF is so important.

Our promise

Investing in yourself begins today. Your future self will thank you.

And we'd like to take this moment to congratulate you. Congratulations on wanting more for yourself and your family. Congratulations on taking the steps to learn how to gain more from your life. Congratulations on making the commitment to invest in yourself. Learning takes time, and as you'll soon discover, you really are worth it.

CHAPTER 1

Principle 1: Wake Up Excited for the Day—An Art and a Practice

Everywhere you turn—both online and offline—people are talking about the importance of having a positive mental attitude. There are books on the subject, YouTube videos, and even life coaches preaching the benefits and power of positive thinking.

Spoiler alert: We agree 100%. A key ingredient to achieving anything in life, especially achieving your goals, is a positive mental attitude.

Waking up excited for the day ahead has a direct impact on the outcome of any day—again, we agree. But here's a little detail that no one ever seems to mention: humans are not born with a natural ability to wake up excited for the day ahead. It's just not how we're wired. When you think about it, babies wake up feeling uncomfortable and cry to get the attention of their parents. Unable to express themselves with words, their cries speak volumes about hunger, a diaper that needs changing, or simply a need to be picked up and cuddled.

Crying in distress is a baby's way of communicating that something is wrong or that they have a need. Not only is crying a habit that we create with our first breath, but it stems from an instinct to survive.

Case in point: on the very first day of our lives, we wake up feeling miserable. Not only that, but we learn to accept this as normal.

Here's a question for you ...

If waking up feeling miserable begins as a need to survive and is then developed into a habit, shouldn't there be a way to change this habit or learn a new one since we can now get up and take care of our own needs? The answer: Absolutely!

Over the course of our years in business and throughout our personal lives, we've discovered that waking up excited for the day—every day—is both an art and a practice. It's a game-changer and something everyone should strive for. It's the first step towards leading a happy life and living the life of your dreams.

The first steps in changing any aspect of our lives—whether it's a habit or circumstance—is awareness and acceptance. First, an awareness that a change must be made. Second, acceptance that we want (and can!) make that change. This acceptance can also be coined as a responsibility. A responsibility to yourself.

Let's face it. Crappy things happen to good people, so waking up excited for the day isn't always as easy as being willing to make a change. While today we admit to being full ambassadors of the benefits of waking up feeling excited for the day ahead, our following stories demonstrate that we also had to learn this new habit. And if we may, it's a habit well worth the effort.

Foster's story

Whether it's my life or someone else's, one thing that I learned very early on is that everybody has problems. In fact, there are as many problems as there are people on this planet. To name but a few, finances, family, health, and childhood experiences that impact our self-worth. And these are just the tip of the iceberg. No matter what challenges you face today, problems are everyone's—for lack of a better word—problem. A fact of life is that problems belong to

Principle 1: Wake Up Excited for the Day—An Art and a Practice

everyone. And if I may, problems are a lesson in character. They're also an opportunity to develop character and grow.

Looking back now after these many years, I can say that my lessons in character began a little early. Too early? I can't speak for the powers that be. Clearly, a plan was in place, and like anyone in the midst of pain and turmoil, there's no way that I could have known that among other lessons, my early years would be a lesson in gratitude.

To give you context of my early life, my first bed was a mat. Not a mattress, but a mat. And I'm not talking about a yoga mat either. I was born and raised in a small village in West Africa called Bosuso. My bed was hand-woven and made from sticks and palm branches. Although I didn't know the difference at the time, I can say the following with a pure heart: my place for sleep was not made for comfort. But it was a bed—my bed. Situated on the floor in my parents' bedroom next to my mother, I really had nothing to complain about. Especially since at the time of this memory, I was seven years old, and as it is for anyone at that tender age, being next to one's dear mother is always the best place in the world.

Here's a glimpse into my early life.

Evenings were spent with my grandmother, with whom we lived, my parents, and my siblings: two brothers and two sisters. Eight people living in a small hut.

Regardless of our poor living conditions, we had a loving family life, and for that I will be forever grateful. Mealtimes were spent as a family. Along with our chores, we had time to play with the other children in the neighborhood. Our evening routine consisted of washing ourselves to get ready for bed, followed by time spent together on the veranda listening to our grandmother and mother tell us stories. Looking back now, it was a precious part of the day and I believe we all knew it, even back then.

My grandmother was a fish merchant. Today we would call it her "line of work," but really, it was her way of contributing to the family's survival. We didn't have a fridge, so she would smoke the raw fish every evening to dry it so that it was preserved and ready for the next day's walk to the market.

Along with listening to family stories, my siblings and I would spend our evenings doing our part in shelling nuts from palm kernels. As young as we were, my siblings and I, we played a big part in the family chores; we had our responsibilities. No complaints here. It was our way of life.

Prior to bedtime we would read from the Bible. And while we didn't have much, nothing was ever taken for granted. Everything was a blessing, and duly respected and recognized as so.

Then came the night of October 10, 1970. The night that changed everything.

My father was away for work and I was sleeping on my mat on the floor next to my mother's bed when suddenly something woke me up. Wide-eyed yet groggy, I remained lying on my mat in the dark, slowly realizing that moans and groans were coming from just above me. My mother was struggling, pain escaping in screams, as blood dripped from her mattress onto the ground next to me.

I quickly rushed to my grandmother's room for help. As I'm sure you can imagine, seeing my mother drenched in her own blood had me panic-stricken; I had no idea what to do. Upon seeing what was happening, my grandmother quickly woke my siblings while hollering at me to knock on the door of the schoolteacher who was renting a room in our hut. He and I immediately set off on foot to the nearest health center in our village. In today's terms, the health center would be the equivalent of a clinic. Since we lived in a small village, there were no hospitals nearby.

The schoolteacher and I managed to get an ambulance, a little Volkswagen van, to drive to our house to take my mother to the nearest hospital. Pregnant, she was clearly suffering from complications.

That night in her room, seeing her in pain and lying in her own blood, was the last time I ever saw my mother. She died in the ambulance on the way to the hospital. Unknown to any of us at the time, my father would join her seven years later, not long after my 14th birthday.

Before we get to that story, I want to take this opportunity to give credit to my grandmother. She was my mother's mother, and as I'm sure you can imagine, she would have given anything—including her own life—to spare the life of her youngest child.

My grandma Christina was a very loving woman. She did everything she could to look after us and help provide for us. We in turn, my siblings and I, did what we could. Growing up, we didn't have running water or a flushing toilet. Every morning we would fetch the daily water, transporting it in a bucket that we carried on top of our heads. That's right. Those pictures you see of African children carrying buckets of water on their heads while walking barefoot are a true depiction, and it was our way of life. About ten trips were required to make sure that our grandmother had enough water to do her chores for the day while we were at school. This was our morning routine.

Then one hot afternoon we got the news that our father had been rushed to the hospital. This came as quite a shock, partly because we had never seen our father sick, but mostly because somewhere inside of us existed an unspoken belief that after our mother's passing, nothing bad could or should ever happen to our family again.

The speculation around my father's death was that he may have suffered a heart attack. The difference between my mother's death and my father's is that I was able to see my father's body after his demise. In contrast, when our mother died seven years earlier, it had been a family decision that my baby sister and I should not see our mother during her funeral. I realize now that it was an attempt to protect us, since we were so very young at the time.

"Don't worry, you'll see your mom again." Words spoken to us by our aunties and uncles and meant to console us. And an attempt to keep our innocence from being swallowed by a tragedy no child should have to endure. Even though I didn't understand what was truly happening, part of me believed everything they said.

It wasn't until my father's death during my early teenage years that it suddenly dawned on me that my mom and now my dad were truly gone forever. I would never again hear their voices, see their smiles, feel their touch. It was during this time of grieving for my father that I began to question everything.

The words that echoed in my mind—"they're in a better place"—made no sense to me. How could my parents be in a better place without us; without my grandma Christina, without my siblings and me?

Who is behind all this?

During Sunday school lessons we learned about an "afterlife." It was described as a place where you went to meet Jesus after death, and that's where my parents had gone. But both as a young child and as an adolescent on the brink of manhood, I found it very difficult to understand this. I didn't realize it at the time, but the questions that haunted me were growing into a vortex of silent anger.

Principle 1: Wake Up Excited for the Day—An Art and a Practice

Before entering high school, I had applied to enter the military academy and was accepted. Fortunately for me and possibly fate itself, my older brother, David, recognized my anger and stepped up with a parental rebuff. He knew that my having access to weapons with an angry heart could only lead to trouble. Conscious of it or not, I believed that my parents had been unfairly taken away from us. And while I may have been too young to realize it, my brother recognized my growing irate need for revenge. What I may or may not have done, we'll never know. Today my brother and I laugh at the memory. If you can imagine a 16-year-old version of me, angry at the world, and if you know me in person, I'm certain you'll agree, it is laughable.

Thinking back on everything that I went through as a child, I believe that it has rounded me off and given me an appreciation for life. It has also provided me with a sense of gratitude and perspective that I might not otherwise have been able to grasp. Being of African origin and knowing that I didn't have any of the things that my three children have today, I feel grateful for my ability to provide them with the lifestyle that we enjoy. As a minor example, my daughter (who at the time of this writing is 18 years old) has always had her own bedroom, something unheard of during my childhood in West Africa.

Of course, when I tell my kids the stories of my own upbringing and share the contrast of a life that they have never been exposed to (the hardships, the fact that there was never enough food, how we had no concept of running water and plumbing, how I was 12 years old before I got to sleep on a real mattress), they see it as a way for me to discipline them or as if I'm trying to get tough on them. Frankly, I'm just trying to demonstrate how fortunate they truly are. I would even use the word "privileged" because in today's world, there are still people that don't ever have leftovers to waste, simply because there is never enough food on the table. We are blessed beyond belief. This is something that my childhood years can never let me take for granted, and for that I am truly grateful.

***

Meanwhile, during another time, in another part of the world, John went through his own darkness. It's hard to understand the experiences that we go through—especially while we're going through them. Are they life lessons? Is the bigger goal to help us grow?

In John's case, his testing grounds surrounded the death of his unborn child.

John's story

John met his wife, Josée, in the early part of 2002. As it is for many couples, the order of their lives together fell into a natural rhythm. They met. Fell in love. Got married. Conceived their first child together. It was an exciting, happy time for their growing family, which also included Josée's daughter from a previous relationship, and whom John immediately loved and accepted as his own.

The new baby was due in the early part of February—a winter baby—and according to the regular prenatal doctor visits, all was going well. As you can imagine, preparing for the holiday season was even more festive that year. The promise of a new life and happily-ever-after has that effect on people.

Then on New Year's Eve, an occasion usually paired with fresh beginnings and anticipation for a happy future, John and Josée realized that something wasn't right. In fact, something was very, very wrong.

Principle 1: Wake Up Excited for the Day—An Art and a Practice

"In an instant, our joy and excitement had been replaced with the terrible news that our baby had died." As John reflects, his voice cracks from the burden of a heavy sorrow that never truly goes away.

At eight months to term, their baby girl was someone they had come to know ... to fall in love with. Naming her after each of their mothers, they were forced to deliver their lifeless child. It was December 31, 2002, when little Alice Diane was induced into this world. Her silence echoed the emptiness felt by John and Josée. It was one of the darkest and most difficult days of their lives.

"When the doctors confirmed that our baby girl was dead, the news paralyzed us into a painful silence. It was after the delivery when we went back to the house and had to face the bedroom that we had prepared for her that all the emotions gushed out of what seemed like every pore of our essence. I'd had friends and family members pass away throughout my life, but there's nothing like the death of a child. It happens. You hear stories about it. And yet you can't prepare for it.

"When something like this happens, it wears you down. It challenges your faith and makes you question everything that you've always believed in. Some of the questions I found myself asking included, *A baby? Why didn't you take me? Why didn't you take some of the bad guys out there?*" John recalls.

"I went through a period of anger. I was tormented by a strong sense of hatred and resentment. Regardless, all I really had to fall back on was my faith. It was such a difficult time, yet I will say that my friends in the network marketing industry certainly supported us. This is when I truly realized that having a support group is a gift.

"Another thing that helped us get through this was that we—Josée and I—started to fall back on our many years of self-development training. If you've never lost a child or gone through a similar experience, let me assure you that it makes you lose your way. You tell yourself that things happen for a reason. You ask yourself questions that you never imagined yourself faced with. You question your faith. You question your relationships. You question yourself and the reasons why you do anything. It even forces you to question your own existence and purpose in life.

"During such a dark time, there are two things I'll forever be grateful for: my faith and my years of study in self-development, thanks to my business. It was at this time that I would learn that the two are intertwined.

"I've been in the network marketing industry now for over 30 years. It's the only industry I know of that puts focus on the 'self,' that measures success not by the amount of profits you make but by how you grow as a person and how you help others grow.

"After the death of Alice Diane, I went through all the emotions. The confusion. The anger. The resentment. At the same time, my thoughts also led me to reflect on the meaning behind some of the great works I had read over the years. For example, I thought about a book that Jim Rohn wrote years ago called *The Seasons of Life*.

"In his book, Jim uses the metaphor of the four seasons. Spring is a time for optimism and anticipation. The trees, flowers, and grass are growing. You feel good, renewed. Then summer comes along, and what do we do? We prepare. We grow, plan, and organize for the downtime. Fall is a time to harvest and store what we've grown for the upcoming downtime. And of course, winter represents that downtime. Remembering this metaphor made me realize that I was in a wintertime—both on a yearly calendar and in my life as well. It

Principle 1: Wake Up Excited for the Day—An Art and a Practice

also made me realize that eventually the circle would continue and bring me to a time of renewal. Although I couldn't feel it during the darkness of my emotions, I knew it to be true from a mindset of logic.

"The truth is that the death of a child violates the rules of nature. Our kids are supposed to bury us, not the other way around. And, to be honest, this violation challenged the relationship between Josée and me for what seemed like a long time; if not measured on a linear level, certainly in depth. While we were going through this together, we were also going through it apart. But because we kept our faith, our wits, and our belief systems throughout, along with the self-development skills that we had acquired over the years, I can say today that we managed to make it through. Thankfully.

"To add to that, no matter what you call your maker, mine must have a sense of humor because exactly one year after the death of our baby, and on the exact same day—December 31—our son, Fred, was born. A time of winter on the calendar year once again, but this time representing a time of optimism and hope. Spring had come our way, bringing with it a gift: our baby boy.

"From a self-development standpoint, there are life situations and events that you have no control over and that challenge you. I'm not promoting any one belief system or religion, but I'll certainly promote faith, because you have to believe in something. That something, no matter what it is to you on a personal level, is what helps you through the tough times.

"There are some circumstances that stay with you forever. To this day, even after all these years, we heal a little bit more and we do it as a family. Two of our children born on the same day, one gone and one very much alive. Every year on December 31 we celebrate Alice in the morning and then we celebrate Fred in the afternoon. It's our way of honoring both of these children—one that we love regardless of our grief, another that brings us joy every single day."

***

We tell you these stories as a reminder that life challenges us all. Regardless of what happened yesterday, it's today that counts. We all have choices to make, and one of the most important choices you can make in terms of how it will impact your life is that of attitude.

It's a known fact that having a plan is the best way to achieve anything, from household chores to building a business. The following are a few suggestions to help you develop a habitual and healthy approach to waking up excited for your day. Done consistently and mindfully, you'll be on your way to creating your new habit!

- Write down what you want to achieve in a week, month, or year.
- Break down your achievements into smaller tasks or steps and then create daily to-do lists that are in line with your greater goal.
- Post weekly or monthly calendars on the wall near your desk or somewhere that you'll see them frequently throughout the day—on your fridge and in your car—anywhere that will help remind you of your goals and tasks.
- Review your upcoming weeks on Sunday evenings or first thing Monday mornings.
- Be aware of the little things:
  - Sunrises/sunsets
  - The sound of children laughing
  - The aroma of morning coffee (oh, and that first sip!)

Principle 1: Wake Up Excited for the Day—An Art and a Practice

- Schedule time to do the things you love, including downtime with your family or simply watching your favorite TV show.
- Read inspirational books. (See the list of recommended reading at the end of this book.)
- Develop a habit of looking for the bright side of any situation and the positive attributes of every person you meet.

CHAPTER 2

Principle 2: Listen to YOUR Reason—It's the Heart of the Matter

Look up the word "vice" in the dictionary and you'll run across definitions that speak about immoral (and even *evil*) habits or practices. You may even stumble on meanings that talk about "a weakness in character." Here's our definition of the word, or better yet, an answer to the question: *What's your vice?*

For us, it has nothing to do with any weakness in character or bad habits, but rather a *force* that drives a person to achieve great things and accomplish well-defined goals. Goals that make a difference and impact not only on the person or group achieving them but also in the lives of everyone around them, including family and friends, and perhaps even in the lives of people they may never meet.

A vice is something that is so important to you personally that it propels you forward, giving you the motivation and inspiration you need to sustain a daily habit while you inch your way forward towards your goal. Depending on what your vice is, that daily habit could be anything from morning walks to help you achieve a health or weight-loss goal, to a daily practice routine for learning how to play an instrument, or maintaining a work habit that enables you to reach that brass ring of success—however you define success.

The key word here is "daily." A vice drives you to achieve, complete, reach. In other words, a "vice" isn't necessarily a bad habit or weakness in character but rather a strength; a driving force, an empowering tool that gives you control of your life. A vice can also be described as a "reason." There are so many reasons why we do the things we do or care about the things we care about. While we've both achieved success in the same industry with our respective businesses, we do it for very different reasons. In other words, we're both driven by our own individual vices.

Thoughts from John ...

If I compare my reason for doing what I do today with my reason from 30 years ago, my motives may have gone through a few iterations, but really, I'm driven by the same goal today as I was back then. Back then I had bills to pay. I had to make a living. Today I still have bills to pay. I still have to make a living. Fundamentally, people like to associate emotional validations with why they start a business. But the reality is that in 1983 I needed to make a living in order to support myself. And just like everyone else, today I still need to support myself and my family.

I was just getting out of college when I first started my network marketing business. About a month prior to graduating, I was looking for a job when I discovered the network marketing business model purely by accident. Luckily for me, I started making money almost immediately. To give you an example, during my first weekend in the business, I sold $800 worth of product and made about $320 in profits. Thirty years ago, that was a lot of money. Consider it a supplemental earning for someone who has a full-time job and today it's still a lot of money. This gave me confidence. It proved to me that if worse ever came to worst, I could at least sell something that I believed in.

So here we are today, and the bills are a lot bigger because I have a family now; but fundamentally, the reason that drives me hasn't changed. I still need to make a living. I have two kids that are very engaged in two of the most expensive sports: figure skating and hockey. Both my kids are privately coached. In my son's case, he goes to a hockey academy, and my daughter is coached by an Olympic champion. And I'm proud to say that I can afford to give them what they need to follow their dreams and passions—all because I followed mine and continue to do so.

My point is that if you're going to afford to give your family the best that you can and the best that they deserve, be it education or in this case sports education, these things cost money. You'll hear talk of emotional reasons, and there's nothing wrong with that. In fact, if it gives you courage and motivation, more power to you. At the same time, I want to point out that necessity is also an empowering reason. I was on my own at a fairly young age. And while I had some family assistance here and there, for the most part I had no choice but to earn a living on my own.

One thing that I'm grateful for is that I learned how to employ myself at a very young age. When I was 14 years old, I did lawn work for people in my neighborhood. During the summer months, I cut lawns. I picked up acorns in the fall. And during the winter months I shoveled snow. Looking back now, I somehow learned at a young age how to scope out opportunities. I also recognize this as something you either have or you don't. And if you don't, the good news is that it's a life skill that can be developed. Eventually I wound up having to hire people, and many of them were older than I was at the time.

When I went away to college, everything changed for me simply because I moved away from where I had been brought up and I ended up giving up that income. In hindsight, that was probably foolish. Looking back, I should have—and could have—kept that business going. As they say, you live and learn.

Network marketing came along by accident when a buddy of mine with whom I trained in wrestling introduced me to this particular business model. It made complete sense to me from day one. And to be perfectly frank, it wasn't like I was some grandiose business expert. I just needed something—a product—to sell, and that particular network marketing business at the time had something I could believe in. It provided me with a way into the business, and more than that, it gave me an opportunity to further develop my entrepreneurial talents.

Now, going back to that first weekend and my initial success, would I have kept with it if I hadn't made just over $300? Was it just dumb luck? I'll never know. Sometimes I wonder if the fact that I did make that much money so early in the game wasn't somehow a godsend, because since that very first weekend in the business, I've had the opportunity to give back by helping a lot of other people throughout the years.

So, while the dollar figure was good for me in that it gave me an incentive to continue, the trickle-down effect was that it drove me to help others. As it turns out, my original reason—what started off as simply a necessity to earn a living—turned into something much bigger and more meaningful than I'd envisioned.

Sometimes we do things without realizing how important they are or the impact we're making at that time. We wake up in the morning with an intention to get through our to-do list, and we're so focused on the tasks that we don't often see the big picture until years down the road when we realize that something we believed in was actually contagious and was giving others a purpose as well. Today we call this "finding our tribe."

Optimism: A tool for staying motivated

For my first year of college I went away to Western Pennsylvania. I had some scholarship money, but basically my parents couldn't afford for me to be there, and I returned home after my father had a heart attack. This is when my parents and I realized that I really needed to be back in New Jersey.

At the time, I needed a vehicle, and the only thing I could afford to buy was a mail jeep. I'll never forget this. It cost me $1,000 and, if you can imagine, this less than glamorous vehicle became my means for getting to and from college. It was affordable, but there were a couple of negatives that came along with that. First of all, it only had one seat. I couldn't ask a girl to go out on a date with me, because if I did, where would she sit? Secondly, that single seat was on the wrong side of the vehicle.

This was also the vehicle that I drove when I began my network marketing venture. Again, with a keen eye for opportunities, I took that vehicle and, as ridiculous as anyone could feel driving around in a mail jeep, I managed to turn this negative into a positive. Keeping in mind that UPS wasn't what it is today, we got products for our growing business through air freight. We would have our shipments sent to Newark Airport, and I would drive to the airport with my mail truck and pick up everyone's orders for a small fee of 3% of whatever their individual orders were. Everyone from my group appreciated this because I was providing a service that was convenient for them. On my side, I had created a sub-business from my initial business. The profit wasn't life-changing, but I had managed to give a positive spin to the sometimes awkward fact that I was driving a mail jeep.

When life isn't perfect (and let's face it, it rarely is), it's so easy to focus on the negative aspects of our circumstances. In my case, I was driving a clunky vehicle, and to be quite frank, everyone saw that. It wasn't even a "crappy" vehicle. It was a mail truck. One usually driven solely by vocation. And I didn't buy it to create a profit center. I bought it out of necessity. It was all I could afford, and I needed something to get to and from school.

And here, as awkward or unconventional as it looked, that mail truck became an asset. Suddenly I was able to build my business faster because people had a regular delivery date as a motivating factor. They would think, "If I can get my products on Wednesday, I can sell my inventory and reorder right away."

To demonstrate the win-win aspect, without this pick-up and delivery service that I was providing, my team and network of customers would have let their products sit at Newark Airport to be picked up at their earliest convenience (usually the following Saturday). That mail truck created a momentum and flow for moving products. And at the rate I was charging, which was reasonable, products sold very quickly, which meant that my group volume was increasing significantly faster. Admittedly, I was young at the time and had no idea how beneficial this little service of mine was to everyone, including me.

As a general rule, people often only focus on the negative. But I share this story to demonstrate that if you look at things the right way, you'll always find an opportunity buried in there somewhere. In many ways, this is a learned habit. We're not born with the inclination to look for or focus on the positive side of things. In fact, quite the opposite. This is a habit that we need to consciously develop and nurture.

Maintaining momentum: A game I play

There is a competitive edge to the network marketing business model that has always appealed to me. Almost like sports, I like to push myself a little further every day. For example, when I first got started in my business, I would challenge myself from month to month to see if I couldn't do a little better.

As I mentioned, making money was initially a necessity. I started with a goal to make $1,000 a month, because that was what I needed to pay my basic bills. Once I reached that on a consistent basis (which was fairly quickly), my next goal was $1,500. Then $2,000. At that time, I was thinking in increments of $500 a month, and the question I asked myself was always the same: "What can I do next to challenge myself?"

For me, it started as an eye for spotting opportunities and a game of challenging myself to always do a little better. That's what worked for me and continues to drive my reason for success. For Foster, it's very different, and I love that because it demonstrates that there are as many reasons and opportunities to succeed as there are people in the world.

Thoughts from Foster ...

I've always had a clear vision of what I wanted for myself: to be my own boss. And it's this clarity that has been the driving force behind my reasons for staying motivated. If I may put gratitude first, I consider myself blessed to have found a career that brings me fulfillment on every level, while providing me with a sense of purpose and means for earning an income.

Unfortunately, most people go to work every day for the primary reason of earning a paycheck and paying bills. Do they enjoy their work? Do they find satisfaction in it? Do they feel that they're contributing to their personal sense of fulfillment? The answer to these questions is no. And yet, the vast majority of people, no matter where they live, want to be happy and successful in their work lives. The disconnect here is that most people are not able to define what happiness or success is *for them*selves as individuals.

I truly believe that when you know what you want out of life—when you can get a clear picture in your mind—you get a better sense of your true purpose, which in turn gives you the tools to be much more than what you currently are. When you are more, you get more. Not just in material possessions, although this organically falls into it as well. What I'm referring to here is more of a sense of inner satisfaction. It all comes down to knowing and understanding what you want out of life and your place in the overall big picture. The other benefit to a clear definition of what you want is that it gives you the energy and momentum for staying motivated! This has been my secret all along.

There's a direct link between people that are genuinely happy and how they feel about their work, whether they view it as a job or as a career. You can be a teacher, a dentist, a school janitor, or an entrepreneur. Whatever your work, when you love what you do, it has a direct impact on your overall sense of joy.

Genuine success is all about becoming the person you were meant to be by achieving your dreams. And as we know, dreams are different for everyone. I am clear on my reasons for doing what I do. And I've noticed that because of this, I am more willing to overcome any obstacles along the way. This is because a strong reason becomes the fuel that pushes you forward. If my definition for what I want out of life was vague, the answers to many of the questions that arise on my journey towards success would also be vague.

Another belief I have is that every single person on this planet has a purpose and a mission in life. The challenge for many people is in figuring out what their purpose is. While I wasn't always sure of the details, I've always known that I wanted to work for myself—to do things my way. When I was introduced to the network marketing business model, I signed on right away because I knew this was the opportunity that would lead me to making a difference.

While network marketing is the means for me to be my own boss, it's also the medium for me to work with and help other people. This is so important for me, and the fact that this is what I get to do every single day of my life is a great feeling. In itself, it's a feeling of achievement. It's also what leads me to be what I call "a producer" and high achiever.

A person with a strong reason or strong "why" makes a positive difference in the world—both in the lives of their immediate family and in making a contribution to something bigger than themselves. A clear reason will bring the best out of you. It moves you beyond settling for mediocrity. It's a driving force.

Unlimited Opportunity

One of the many aspects that I love about my network marketing business is that it gives me that all-important sense of unlimited opportunity. There is no glass ceiling. The word "unlimited" says that you're a part of something that's bigger than yourself. It's about people. It's about doing things according to your own set of values.

It's about presenting opportunities to others. It's about sharing ideas and developing, not only as an individual but as a team. And then, of course, there's the fact that you're providing products to people that need them: products that people use, products that you yourself believe in.

Even within the context of an unstable economy, as long as you're putting your best foot forward and sincerely working at growing your business, you can never get fired or lose your job because you are in control of your own success.

Attracting the Right Team

There's a strong relation between your messaging and your target audience or what you're selling and what people are buying. Take my network marketing business as an example. It's built on a foundation of health. And while there are many products on the market that promote a healthy lifestyle, my entire business—from the products to the messaging to the relationship that I have with my team—is based on health. Said another way, people don't just buy into what you sell; they buy into what you do and what you believe in. Your integrity, your morals, and your principles.

So, while everyone appreciates good health, what sets my products apart from other products is that my business is based on a reason and a purpose. In other words, a driving force where my "why" resonates with other people's why. People look for something that is far better than just any other product on the market. They want to relate to *the message*.

Putting the onus back on you, the reader, success in any endeavor will always be driven by the reason behind what you do. Figure out why you want to do something, and you've figured out

Principle 2: Listen to YOUR Reason—It's the Heart of the Matter

your purpose. And your purpose—your *why*—is always bigger than you. This is what makes it a driving force.

Let's take Martin Luther King as an example. Why did so many people show up that day in Washington to hear him give his speech, "I have a dream" on that day? They showed up because his message resonated with them. They showed up because his message was their message.

A few questions to ask yourself

Have you discovered your purpose in life?

If so, what is it?

Write a statement about why you do what you do for a living.

Are you doing what you are doing for a living because you *have to* or because you *want to*?

Write a statement to describe your passion for either your current job or your dream job.

If you had a chance to do a career makeover, what changes would you make?

What changes can you implement now?

Do you have any bad habits you'd like to break in order to make room for good habits that bring you closer to your goals?

CHAPTER 3

Principle 3: Instill the Right Mindset–And You'll Have no Choice but to Succeed

What is my mindset?

This is one of the most important questions you can ask yourself. And while you may think you have a clear understanding of your mindset, what it means, and its impact on your life, it's worthwhile to take some time to really think about it.

Based on your beliefs—about yourself, your abilities, your strengths, and your capacity to trust your intentions—the wonderful thing about your mindset is that you can set it to achieve whatever results you want in any area of your life. A good avatar to help describe mindset is the Marvel Comics character, the Hulk. You realize while watching him in action that there are no obstacles that can stop him because he's fixated on one thing, consumed by determination.

More than a simple question, "What is my mindset?" is one of reflection; a conscious decision that stems from a determination to achieve a goal, regardless of any obstacles or hindrances, just like the Hulk.

We see this often when individuals with perceived hindrances attain incredible results. Think Stephen Hawking. Although physically limited due to motor neuron disease (also known as Lou Gehrig's disease), this didn't stop him from pursuing his achievements, including his work in physics and his writings. Despite his disability and perceived "limitations," Hawking was even known for his sense of humor. Despite his obstacles, Hawking made a huge impact on our understanding of the universe. But you don't have to be a genius like Stephen Hawking to achieve great things. You just need the right mindset.

Thoughts from John ...

The right mindset is the idea that you're either going to the top of the mountain where you'll wave to everyone with a sense of achievement, or you'll be dead at the bottom. I've used this analogy for years, and it's how I've lived every aspect of my life, whether we're talking about athletics or business.

Using the Olympic Games as an example, the only place that matters is first place. It's the same for hockey, football, baseball, or basketball. First place or no place at all. This is not to say that people who don't achieve first place are inferior to the ones that do. What it does mean is that the people who embrace a mindset of getting to the top level of whatever they're endeavoring to do—whether it's sports, business, or the arts—that's where they're headed. No forks in the road; just one direction.

I go back to Vince Lombardi, who was not only one of the greatest football coaches, but also a philosopher of sorts with degrees in sciences. Lombardi was misquoted when a reporter repeated him as having said "winning is the only thing." He later got the opportunity to correct the reporter, stating that his point was that *endeavoring to win is the only thing*. Do you see the difference? And again, this goes back to mindset.

The truth is that we're not always going to achieve everything in life that we set out to accomplish. While I haven't achieved

Principle 3: Instill the Right Mindset—And You'll Have no Choice but to Succeed

everything that I've set out to do, I have achieved specific goals because I sincerely worked to get to the top. About ten years ago I remember watching a young basketball player, a kid at the time, carry his team on his back. This had a huge impact on me, and I spoke to my mentor, Larry Thompson, about it. I didn't realize it, but at the time I was witnessing this guy's mindset and the true source of what he would come to accomplish in the NBA. You could just see that he was not going to give up. This great athlete and player turned out to be the man we know today as the great LeBron James.

As mentioned, my own mantra has always been "top of the mountain or dead at the bottom." Anything in between is unacceptable. What you seek is what you need to work toward—without integrating the word "try" in your vocabulary. Are you always going to succeed? Honestly, no. But if you don't endeavor to win, if you don't have the mindset of a champion, you're not going to achieve anything.

If you have the mindset of a "loser," you're going to lose. If you have the mindset of a winner, you may not get the gold medal, the Stanley Cup ring, or the top rank in your company. But by endeavoring and having the right mindset to get whatever it is you want to achieve, you're going to get something better than if you didn't have the right mindset.

In my own life, I was in high school when I started to endeavor to do things. And because of my mindset, I was a very good athlete and achieved some huge goals.

Unfortunately, I wound up getting hit in the back during a football game and couldn't fully achieve what I wanted to because of the impact this had on my physical health.

However, I was able to reset my mind to do other things within athletics which I was ultimately able to learn, including judo, jujitsu, wrestling, and powerlifting. The point is that while I wasn't able to accomplish what I had originally set out to do, I was able to turn my focus and achieve other things with the same amount of passion. The mindset never changes in terms of the way you think. That said, what does change are the goals or the achievements within the modifications that you have to make due to the confines of health, finances, or circumstances.

The point I want to make—and this is very important—is that the mindset of a champion never changes. Nor does it change as we get older. It may change from the athletics field to the business world, as an example, but the way you think, the way that you set your mind to accomplish something, never alters.

The question I'm often asked is, "How does a nonachiever change their mindset so that they can start thinking like an achiever?" Well, my answer to that is to study what other people have done. Specifically, people who have achieved what you want to achieve.

It's been said that if you want to get rich, study money. If you want to become a champion, study champions; study people who have achieved. And study people who have achieved but may not have had the right circumstances to achieve, who managed it anyway.

A great example of this is Nelson Mandela, someone I consider to be one of the greatest champions of the world. Even though he was put in jail for many, many years, he never gave up on his vision for his country. And he didn't only want to do it for his own people, he wanted to do it collectively for the people of South Africa. This is a powerful example under the most difficult of circumstances.

Looking at biblical times, Paul was someone who transformed his life. He started out as a murderer of Christians, who later

Principle 3: Instill the Right Mindset—And You'll Have no Choice but to Succeed

changed his mindset to do only good things for the remaining years of his life. In terms of modern examples, triathlete Dick Hoyt had the mindset to not only drag himself to practice, but also bring his son who had a physical disability with him as well.

All that to say that if you're sitting there with two arms and two legs and good health and you're not doing anything with your life, whose fault is that? It comes down to not only finding ways to motivate yourself with your mindset but also finding good examples of people who are doing and achieving in spite of their circumstances. When you study these people, the first thing you're going to realize is that they have self-responsibility. They don't make excuses for why things aren't happening the way they want them to happen. Instead, they take responsibility for their lives. And as a result, the rest of us on the outside can't help but be in awe at their achievements *in spite* of their circumstances. Once again, it is a matter of overcoming obstacles with the right mindset and constantly making sure that our focus is on winning.

Another great example of someone who motivated me at a young age is a man named Dan Gable, who not only was an Olympic champion in wrestling but was unbeaten in 181 matches during his high school and college years. Gable lost his last collegiate match, believe it or not, then rededicated himself. This is someone who was already at the top of his profession with multiple national championships in wrestling, and he rededicated himself for the Olympics by training seven hours every day. During the 1972 Olympics, he not only won but he did not give up a point in doing so. How did he accomplish this? Once again, he found the mindset within a very difficult circumstance.

While on a trip with his parents when he was younger, his sister had stayed home because she had to work. It was during this time that she was brutally murdered. This left Dan as an only child, and in many ways, responsible for keeping his parents' marriage together. Can you imagine the stress of something like that? The best of people wouldn't wish this on their worst enemy! Yet, he took this tragedy and somehow managed to let it drive him. He is even reported to have said, "The more you can settle into focusing on what you have and what you would like to do and where you want to go—a positive point of view—the quicker things turn around and positive things start to happen,"

The best thing you can do for yourself is to find people that are champions. Surround yourself with people who achieve in spite of themselves and their circumstances, whether their limitations are physical, mental, financial, or even political in some cases. Many people who come from countries where they don't have the freedom that we do here in North America are able to do wonderful things with their lives. This is important, but not for the reasons that first come to mind. While accomplishing great things provides a sense of accomplishment for the person achieving them, the best part is that accomplishing wonderful things inspires others!

Going back to when I was 17 years old and lying in the hospital with an injury that would change the course of my life, I suddenly found myself without a perceived future. I went from knowing exactly what I wanted to achieve in life to not knowing if I was ever going to walk again. Did I make excuses? No. Did I continue to hold myself accountable? Yes.

And what helped me rediscover that in myself was the book *The Power of Positive Thinking* by Dr. Norman Vincent Peale, which I highly recommend.

One of the things I remember reading in that book are Peale's thoughts on tranquility. This relates to the super achievers we hear about, whether they're training for an Olympic gold medal or other endeavor, competing at the highest level, or becoming the brain surgeon who's going to save your life. The one commonality among all of them is that they are calm. They are tranquil. They have an emotional state of calm that most of us strive for.

These achievers are realists. They see the circumstances in front of them and they don't have rose-colored glasses. What they do is figure out a way to shift their paradigms in the right direction. While this may seem like a skill that only a few can master, it's really all about being aware, being focused, and having the right mindset. The good news is that these are skills we can all learn.

Thoughts from Foster ...

I left Ghana in May of 1986 to come to North America because it was perceived to be the land of opportunity. I didn't really know anything more than that. For a young man like me, it was a scary time in my country. I felt limited. I felt that I would never be able to break the pattern, so I had it in my head that I needed to leave and move to North America.

That said, it wasn't an easy thing to do. I was in my early 20s and leaving meant that I was not only leaving a country in political turmoil but that I was also leaving my family and friends behind. It was very difficult, and I had mixed feelings. I was sad to leave my loved ones behind, yet excited about the prospect of making it to America and discovering this land of opportunity.

Up until I was 24 years old, I had never lived anywhere else; I had never traveled. So naturally I had a sense of national and cultural pride. Ghana gave me a sense of love and belonging. All the people that I loved and that loved me unconditionally ... this is what I was leaving behind. There was an overshadowing possibility of never seeing any of them again, because nobody ever knows what tomorrow will bring. As positive as I was, I had no crystal ball, no way of knowing if I would ever see my family and friends again.

I had never been on an airplane before, so the anticipation of boarding a plane was exciting. Today, I also recognize the amount of courage it took for me to do something that I'd never experienced, while knowing that I was about to travel for about 14 hours in the air. I'd be lying if I said that it wasn't scary.

Once I arrived in Canada, I had many obstacles, including the immigration process. It took time for me to get my work permit and to become a citizen. Meanwhile, I learned to take whatever was available to me and to just make the best of every situation.

I chose to come to Canada because it was perceived as a lovely country, very peaceful and a place where every race was accepted and respected. I just knew that Canada could be a place I could eventually call home, and everything that I had read and studied about Canada before embarking on my journey was so positive.

To this day, I believe that it was a good choice. Fortunately for me, I had an older brother who had already been here for about five months before I arrived, and he was able to confirm a lot of what I had already read about this great country.

My first job was in Montreal, and it was a routine job where I worked on an assembly line. I remember going through a lot of mixed emotions during that time. I would have these inner dialogues with myself where I wasn't so much questioning if I'd made the right decision to leave my home in Ghana but was more asking myself, *what's next?*

I was always seeking and curious to know what else was available to me. Every time I asked the question, I listened for the response.

Principle 3: Instill the Right Mindset—And You'll Have no Choice but to Succeed

There was this voice that was always reminding me that I could do better, that there was something better out there for me.

This mindset has led me to where I am today. And if someone were to ask me where it comes from, I'd have to answer with an assumption: I believe it's always been a part of who I am. I think back to my high school days in Ghana and remember how I made the decision to learn how to repair shoes. This turned into work that I did for a long time. And something that surprised me along the way was that I always had money. Most of the time, I had more money coming in than my two brothers, who worked for other people at the time.

That's when I realized that even though it wasn't what I would call a "fun" job, the people coming to me to fix their shoes provided an opportunity. It was cheaper for them to pay me to fix their shoes than to buy a new pair. It was obvious to me that there was a market for repairing shoes, and I was making money with this. I believe to this day that the opportunity for me to make money this way was in many ways preparing me for the future.

Later, during my college years, my brothers and I would paint people's homes, and we would put on this show about how we were professional painters. We did quite well with this.

When I came to North America, I was convinced that there would be opportunities, and my mindset alone opened doors for me. Network marketing was a door opener to freedom, and as I've always loved the idea of working for myself, I jumped on the opportunity.

I've always believed that when you have hope, you can get help. When you give up on yourself, you've given up on hope. Thankfully, I've never given up on hope or on myself. No matter what situation I would find myself in, I always managed to run into the right people or opportunity for that time.

This leads me to the concept of gratitude. I never take anything for granted. A good example of this is that in Ghana, when someone wishes you good, it's not something that is taken lightly. While Canada has truly been a blessing for me, I view my origins in Ghana as being beneficial in that my roots have taught me to appreciate even the smallest of gestures and circumstances. It's been shown to me over the years that gratitude is an important aspect of mindset.

CHAPTER 4

Principle 4: Create Balance—It's the Key to Staying on Track

You've heard the term before: work-life balance. Some people will tell you that it's important; that without it, you risk burning out. Others say that there's no such thing; that if you're not focused on a single specific goal, it's impossible to achieve success. The truth is that what works for you may not work for someone else. This is because "success," as we've mentioned, means different things to different people.

The real formula for identifying a work-life balance is based on a variety of elements, including your priorities, your goals and objectives, and your individual definition of success. And while we believe that a sense of work-life balance is important, we've learned from working with others, as well as from our own personal experiences, that finding what works for you can take time. This is because for the most part, figuring out what works for you is a matter of trial and error.

Almost every successful person has something to say about the topic of work-life balance. And while it's interesting to read about how others manage their life, especially if they've achieved the dream life you envision for yourself, we can pretty much guarantee that an exact replica of anyone else's methodology, philosophy, and approach on balance won't work for you. Our advice is to read a lot on the subject. Adopt what works for you and ignore what doesn't.

Eventually, you'll find the right approach to work-life balance for your individual needs. It is in this spirit—of peeking into the minds and lives of others—that we are happy to share our thoughts and mindsets on the subject.

Thoughts from John ...

What's always worked for me is to ensure that my life coincides with my business. I could easily say the opposite: that my business coincides with my life. This, to me, is interchangeable and represents a work-life balance that I can easily manage.

I meet a lot of people during my travels and everyday life, and a good analogy for a frequent conversation that I have with people is a game of tennis. It goes like this: I hit a ball to a new acquaintance by way of a question: "Hello, nice to meet you. What do you do?"

They respond by telling me about their line of work, whether they're a chiropractor, a yoga instructor, or a bus driver. The natural inclination is for them to reciprocate the question and ask me about my line of work. This is my opportunity to tell them about my business and product story, what it does, its health benefits, and the science behind why it works, etc.

I've had this kind of casual conversation on my way to business meetings and events, at the gym, during hockey games, and during my daughter's figure skating meets. It's simply me going about my life and growing my business at the same time.

The opposite of this approach is if someone only focuses on increasing their business. This to me is a definite passageway to failure, because if you're only seeing dollar signs in your eyes and you don't take a genuine interest in people by talking to them and getting to know them, they're going to see you as someone who's

Principle 4: Create Balance—It's the Key to Staying on Track

trying to "sell them." No one wants to do business or even give time to someone who isn't sincere.

People who are so single-minded and that focus solely on work with no downtime or hobbies don't fully enjoy their lives. What eventually happens is that they burn out very quickly.

When you incorporate balance into both your personal life and business life, you give yourself the opportunity to enjoy the process. Focusing on work alone leads to stress and feeling stress all the time does not equate to a good quality of life. Now having said that, this doesn't mean that having balance will remove all sources of stress. I get stressed sometimes too, but I also have the balance I need when it comes to my kids and other areas of my life. This has taught me when to put the phone down just as much as when it's time to turn off the television.

Of course, one of the most important challenges of our time is in the way that we coexist with technology. We are truly always connected, and this makes it difficult for some people to distance themselves long enough to be able to give their full attention to other areas of life, whether that's watching a movie at the theater or focusing on their kid's school play.

As a good example, recently I was working very closely with a new person on my team. We worked very hard together, and within just over two months, I helped this new member to achieve diamond status. Not long after that, I was on my way to the gym and made the conscious decision to leave my cell phone in the car. This wasn't because I didn't want to hear from anyone but rather because I decided to make that one hour at the gym "my time." I wanted to focus and enjoy the workout without any distractions. When you put it into perspective, it's only an hour. While technology is very efficient, even if someone just needed a quick yes or no answer, a one-hour delay is not going to change the world. As it turns out, this was a good lesson for my new team member. What I impressed upon him was that even though I have a big business, I'm still able to disconnect and focus on other things, including not always being tied to the phone. He admired this.

Believe it or not, this is actually something I've had to learn and come to terms with. I've had to learn that what is just as important as doing the business is NOT doing the business and having that downtime for other things, whether it's exercise or family activities.

The other negative aspect of growing a business in today's world is that we sometimes miss out on the interpersonal aspect of communication. With email and texting, it's so easy to get lost in digital communication.

To have balance requires a conscious effort. It's easy to get sucked into the vacuum of whatever it is that pulls you in one direction. You need that balance with your family, first and foremost, but secondly with your health, including exercise, nutrition, and even personal relationships.

So you wind up making a fortune, then all of a sudden you get to be 50 or 60 years old and you realize that you're going to give it all back because you neglected your health and are suffering from something that might have been avoided if you'd paid a little more attention to things other than making money. That's where the balance comes in. Admittedly, I've been guilty of this too, but as I get older, I realize that there are other things that you need to pay attention to. And while balance may be hard to attain, one of the great things about the network marketing business model is that it actually encourages balance in terms of fostering personal development and building friendships with your business associates.

Another drawback to being one-dimensional is that if you're only about business all the time, you'll push people away from you instead of towards you. No one is interested in hearing from someone who is always trying to "sell" something.

Thoughts from Foster ...

For me, balance is about being efficient and being able to prioritize while planning your days. I have an approach that has been very beneficial to me that I call my "Six Pack." Basically, this is about compartmentalizing different areas of my life that are important to me. This isn't to say that everyone has six areas of their life that they want to focus on. For some it could be three or even nine.

My six areas are broken down like this:

1. Spirituality
2. Family
3. Business
4. Personal development
5. Healthy lifestyle (nutrition/exercise)
6. Social activities

Everyone has 24 hours in a day, and every single day I have things to accomplish, which I call my daily goals.

1. Spirituality

I like to start my day making sure that my spiritual alignment is in place. A great example is a habit that my wife and I have created and continually share with our children during our family times.

Every morning we drive our kids to school. Once we're all in the car and just before we leave the driveway, we sit in front of our home and we pray. We connect with God and express our gratitude for all of our blessings and ask that He protect our children.

We've taught our children not to shy away from our faith. As Christians, we believe that good things can happen just as easily as bad things and preparing by asking for divine protection and guidance is something we practice daily. I also read the Bible and meditate. This prepares me, grounds me, and helps me to focus.

2. Family

I put great value in knowing when I'm needed. In other words, every morning my wife and I make sure that someone is available to drive our kids to school and pick them up at the end of the day.

I have been blessed because of the business that I'm in. It gives me the opportunity to be flexible when required, including preparing nutritious dinners so that when the kids come home at the end of the day, there's a good meal ready for them.

We've also instilled in our kids an understanding that they must know where they should be on a daily basis. Outside of school and home, they have to be in places that we're aware of. We know exactly where our kids are at all times because this is something that is important to us as parents.

3. Business

When I schedule my workday, it's broken down to a point where I am able to tackle each item. Spiritual is the first thing on the list. Family side, I know that the kids need to get to school. It's a schedule. Then by the time 9 a.m. rolls around, I'm ready to engage, whether it's to contact consultants or follow up to answer questions.

4. Personal development
I have made it a daily habit to spend time on my personal development. Whether it's reading or setting aside a specific time to listen to a message that is going to develop me as a better person. To equip myself, I need to learn from people that have already achieved the things that I'm trying to achieve.

5. Healthy lifestyle (nutrition/exercise)
This is where I incorporate good nutrition and fitness every day. Of course, some days are busier than others, and if I can't go to the gym on a specific day, I have a way to do stretches at home. It's all basic stuff, but something that I consider important. I'll even do a power walk in my home if that's all I can fit in, to help get my heart going.

6. Social activities
Personal relationships with people are very important. Sometimes it's as simple as engaging someone for a cup of coffee. It's not necessarily about seeing them every day or every week. It's simply about sitting with someone and getting to know them. It's amazing how much you can learn from a person. You could know someone for 25 years and think you know them, but simply sitting for an hour and truly listening will teach you a lot about the other person and their perspective.

There's a lot of benefit that comes with that, because if you don't really understand people, sometimes you won't understand why they behave in a certain way. This can affect your business. As an example, some people may look at me and think I work too hard or that I'm too committed. Maybe the perception is that because I come from a poor background with roots in Africa, I feel that my life depends on it.

But truly when I look at my previous business, there was a time when I had to drive from Toronto to North Carolina. That's over 15 hours to go to a seminar or a conference. Back then I didn't have the money to fly anywhere. My point is that if I encounter someone today that is complaining about an event that's only two hours away from their home, my response could make them think that I'm being pompous, but after everything that I've been through, a two-hour drive is nothing.

Today everything is dropped off at your door. In my very first network marketing opportunity, when you placed an order, all your products were delivered to your upline, no matter where they lived—close to you or not. My point here is that when I look at everything I've lived through; it has built character in me. So, if someone complains, it's not that I don't understand their pain. It's that I try to focus on the positive.

While my Six Pack is very important to me and symbolizes the balance and priorities in my life, it's not always easy to maintain. Basic planning is necessary to keep yourself on course. Now that doesn't mean that you don't have flexibility. An expression I like to use is "You can plan a perfect picnic, but it could still rain on that day."

It's important to keep in mind that there are certain things that will always be out of our control. But you also have to understand that certain things can wait. For example, if for some reason a hectic schedule prevented me from doing my complete exercise routine, I would just adjust my day and pick it up again the following day. As long as I create a balance and don't get consumed by one area of my life, I feel better equipped to manage those times that fall out of my control. My way of getting back on track is a matter of prioritizing.

CHAPTER 5

Principle 5: Commit. Or Risk Giving up too Soon

It's a familiar scene. We have a goal, whether it's to lose weight and live a healthier lifestyle or achieve that next level of success in our business or career, and we're just not seeing the results fast enough. Suddenly we're overwhelmed with questions and feelings of self-doubt.

> *"Am I spinning my wheels here?"*
> *"What am I doing wrong?"*
> *"Maybe I'm being unrealistic."*
> *"What if this isn't for me?"*
> *"Am I wasting my time?"*

Sometimes we even start comparing ourselves to others, comparing their achievements to where we are. And we all know what happens once we start doing that, right? We begin to doubt ourselves even more!

Nineteenth-century essayist, lecturer, and philosopher Ralph Waldo Emerson is known to have said, "To be yourself in a world that is constantly trying to make you something else is the greatest accomplishment."

When you think about the meaning of that statement, you realize just how unique you are. Comparing yourself to others actually causes you to cheat yourself of the time you need to focus on how you and your unique talents can contribute to those around you, including society, and even the world in many cases.

Here's another meaningful quote, this time from Zen Shin, "A flower does not think of competing to the flower next to it. It just blooms."

In other words, the flower puts its power (its focus) on simply "being" and naturally doing what it's meant to do in its due time. This too is a powerful statement.

The truth is that more often than not, a person's ability to reach their goals has nothing to do with the actual goal and everything to do with their level of commitment. While some people may say that they're committed (and truly believe that they are when they say it), they're also dealing with conflicting beliefs about themselves and their capacity to achieve their goals. What happens in this case is that their focus becomes diluted. They begin to pay more attention to the distractions. Does this sound like you?

The best way to determine if you're really committed to your goal is by taking a good look at your ACTIONS.

Let's say you want to lose 20 pounds. Are you eating the proper foods? Are you limiting or cutting out junk food? Are you dedicated to a regular exercise routine, whether that's going to the gym, taking a yoga class, or simply scheduling daily walks?

Using business and career goals as another example, do you spend more time daydreaming and talking about your ambitions and vision of success than doing the actual work? In the following pages, John and Foster share their personal experiences and their experience in working with others.

Thoughts from John ...

I've seen people make a commitment to their business where they hang around the flagpole until they eventually find someone that

Principle 5: Commit. Or Risk Giving up too Soon

matches their dedication. They build a strong team, and what ends up happening is that they create an incredible business and source of income.

Unfortunately, I've also seen people give up too soon. A great example that comes to mind is someone that for the sake of privacy we'll call Mike. I recruited Mike several years ago, and in turn, he started building his own team. Through the very nature of this business, there were several offshoots of his team across the United States and the UK. One particular person in Mike's downline, whom we'll call Josh, lived in Utah and had recruited a colleague that he worked with at a car dealership. This colleague went on to become one of the top earners in the industry, building a highly successful empire with his network marketing business.

One day Mike received his annual renewal form, but instead of renewing, he threw it out. He had decided that he didn't want to pay the minimal renewal fee for his distributorship. His thought process?

"So, I've sponsored a few people? I'm not really doing anything with this."

Meanwhile, someone in his downline was busy building an empire. You see where I'm going with this, right? If Mike had just paid his renewal fee, he would have not only secured a high and steady income through Josh and his downline, but he would have reignited his original enthusiasm for the business opportunity. This is one of the biggest and saddest examples of what can happen when you give up too soon. Essentially, when you're not committed to your business.

One of the elements that I look for in a potential candidate is whether or not they are in it for the long term. Are they going to hang around or quit? Are they like most people, or are they motivated? Will they enjoy the business? Will they find it easy to talk to people about it? Will they make it a magical experience? Essentially, is it something that they will want to be a part of for the long run?

And part of that is my job. I'm the one that needs to make it fun for my people. I need to make it simple for them and even add some magic to it. Otherwise, why would they stick around? Perhaps the most important aspect of this industry is that it is a "people business." Not only that, but it encourages continuous self-development. No other industry does that.

On the other hand, regardless of how great the company, its products, and the opportunity are, if you're not a positive person, you're going to have a very hard time building your business. Why would anyone want to work with a negative person? That's not a real question. Think about it. If someone is always stressed about everything, they're not going to attract the right kind of people. And since this really is a people business, that's a critical point. Especially when you consider that making a long-term commitment is precisely what you need for long-term results and success, no matter what your goal is.

This isn't unique to this business. Whether you're in direct selling, real estate, or financial planning, your level of commitment is the critical factor that determines your success. Regardless of what industry you're in, you'll have down days and you'll have great days. That's just life, and you can't blame that on your work or chosen field. What's important is that you learn to stay in the middle. You have to make sure that you keep yourself together no matter the circumstances, good or bad. And that's a learned habit. If you focus on your problems, they get bigger. On the other hand, when you focus on your goal, that's the direction that you go in—without fail.

We all have days when everything seems to be going well; we're sponsoring people and selling products. It's easy to be happy on these days. Then there are other days when you ask yourself if this is ever going to work. Doubts enter your mind in the form of questions, such as, "Am I ever going to be able to make a living from this? Or even a part-time living?"

There are days when you call ten people and none of them will be interested. You simply have to power through. I, personally, just went through an entire week where nothing seemed to go right. The website went down. No one I spoke to was interested. Even my team seemed to not be very active. And I've been in this business for over 37 years. This just goes to prove that bad days happen to everyone—novice or veteran.

Then all of a sudden, the last 48 hours turned around and the only word that popped into my head was "Wow!" One of my new people, a lady from Texas that I've been working with, had a great week. This lady is a total sweetheart and great to work with. Naturally, her success means everything to me. Not just in monetary terms but in a sense of self-satisfaction. It's in working with people like her that I see the meaning behind my work and purpose in life.

My recommendation for anyone that wants to stay committed to their goal is don't get too high and don't get too low. Work at keeping yourself in the middle and just keep moving forward. There's a lot of talk these days about leadership development, and that's exactly what this business is all about. Consistency in leadership is something that cuts the wannabes from the achievers. It's the difference between someone making a six-figure income and someone making a part-time income while they continue working a day job that they don't enjoy.

When it comes to the people that I mentor, I look for responders. I want to give my time to people that respond to the stimulus I give them. If I tell you that throughout my career over the last four decades, I've made several million dollars, do you think that this says I know something about the industry? I've put in the time. I've learned from some of the best. And I've made the money to prove it. Your job is to show up and do what I teach you. We're in the leadership development business, and how do you develop leaders? By committing and staying consistent yourself.

Thoughts from Foster ...

Commitment plays a huge role in any area of life. You can't succeed at anything without being committed to the end result of your vision. It's been said before, but I'll repeat it here:

> *Even the so-called overnight successes take years to achieve the level of success that we see.*

People tend to focus on the outcomes, but it's what happens behind the scenes that really matters. I've broken down my thoughts on commitment into five areas:

1. Why
2. How
3. When
4. What
5. Next

1. WHY
I find that having a reason to commit to something is very helpful, and I call it my "why." Reminding myself of my purpose gives me

something to refer to when I need it. And trust me when I say that we all need reminders. Everyone feels lost occasionally and knowing your why—your purpose—is super helpful in getting you back on track when you deviate or lose your focus.

Over the years I've learned a lot about myself. I give credit to this industry and its focus on self-knowledge through self-development. One thing in particular that I've learned about myself is that my word is solid. When I commit to something or someone, you can count on my 100% engagement. This is important, because life is a roller coaster ride. The business world is not immune to the highs and lows. On the high days you'll feel like you're performing in an extraordinary way. Then, of course, the low days hit. This is true of any industry. This is where your *why* comes in. It helps to keep you in line with your vision of success. It gives you purpose and a reason to keep putting one foot in front of the other, and most importantly, going in the right direction.

Another thing that helps is to have a routine, or tasks that you do every single day. This is a way to stay in the game, even when you start doubting yourself. A good example of commitment is my commitment to my family. I cherish them, and it's important to me that I do everything I can to make sure that I don't fail them. I want to always be a good father and a good husband. To achieve this, there are things that I commit to on a daily basis. I may not always feel 100%, but regardless, I always give my all. This is an important point, since we all have days where we don't feel as motivated or inspired.

The same goes for business. If I'm shooting for recognition—as another example—I will do something that puts me in a position to demonstrate that I'm not just all talk. In a leadership position, you always have to be setting the example.

This takes commitment—to yourself, to your purpose or why, and to the people around you.

2. HOW

The best way to commit to anything is by prioritizing. Everyone gets 24 hours in a day, and the only way to accomplish anything is by knowing what your priorities are and by writing them down. Take away the eight hours required for a healthy sleep pattern and calculate what you're going to do with the rest of your time. How many hours will you devote to family? How many hours will you devote to your business?

In other words, you need to commit to three categories other than sleep, including family time, business hours, and time for yourself. I find that breaking it down this way helps to remove a sense of feeling overwhelmed. For example, you don't have to devote eight straight hours to your business. Breaking up your time helps to keep you at peak performance, which is crucial for staying committed. Again, to achieve this, you need to know yourself.

3. WHEN

Scheduling your tasks involves knowing your "how." As an example, you can set specific times for meetings or calls. This depends on knowing when you're at your best for interacting with others as well as knowing when you should be putting the information out there.

4. WHAT

"What" is all about content. Since this is a relationship business, it's not about how much you know but rather how much you care. Your message is very important, which makes your content important.

As mentioned earlier, this is a people business, and you constantly need to be prospecting. I like to say that "you can either be charming or you can be alarming."

5. NEXT

Along with commitment, your next level is about planning and strategy. Looking ahead to help you decide what your next step should be. As people in business—and more importantly, people who want to build something for themselves and for their families—we are committed to making this happen. In many ways, this is a challenge. A challenge that is embraced by anyone with an entrepreneurial spirit. Even if the future is vague, you know what you want your end result to be. And you can only get there when you are truly committed.

CHAPTER 6

Principle 6: Look Back on Life—There's no Time Like Now to Learn from Your Past

Part of our work while preparing to share our thoughts on this principle included research on what other well-known and inspirational people have said about "the past" and its impact on an individual's future. This includes personal lives and decisions, as well as the influence that a person or group of people can have on societies.

From entrepreneurs to leaders of large corporations, we found many great and inspiring stories, thoughts, and philosophies that reflected the importance of an individual's past experiences. Our findings even included stories of failure that, in hindsight, played an integral part of an individual's process for attaining success—viewpoints that demonstrate how paying attention to the past can prevent horrors from reentering a person's life.

That said, nothing quite represented our thoughts on the subject of looking back on our individual pasts. At first this came as a surprise to us. Not because we consider ourselves more "unique" than others. As the expression goes: *"I am unique. Just like everybody else."* But rather, our surprise was more about bringing us to the conclusion that while life experiences will differ from individual to individual, they will always lead to forks on the path that make up a life journey.

This chapter focuses on these forks, because whether you go right or left, and depending on your choices at these forks, when you look back, they will determine whether you've led a successful life, or one filled with regrets.

Leveraging a specific life experience for a better future begins at every fork in your life's road. Lucky for us—lucky for ALL people—life is filled with forks in the road. Whether you're 25 or 65, our hope is that you, reading these words right now, will come to the understanding that a better tomorrow begins with you in the present moment. Our hope is that by sharing our thoughts, you'll come to the next fork in your road and welcome it as an opportunity for committing to the decision that's right for you and right for everyone whose life you will surely impact.

It is our belief that no one is an island. We learn from each other. We encourage each other. We support each other. This is the very reason behind our "why" for writing this book.

Thoughts from John ...

A recent personal experience taught me that looking back on life, no matter where you are in terms of age, growth, or self-development, can help you learn from your past and leverage your experiences. My wife and I, against our better judgment, decided to help a boy that someone very close to us was dating. For the purposes of this book, we'll call the couple Jack and Jill. When I say, "against our better judgment," the truth is that we never liked this boy. Regardless, we helped this young couple out by lending them the money they needed to put a down payment on a house.

On the one hand, we felt sorry for the boy. He had no money, and from our perspective, no real future. On the other hand, a little

Principle 6: Look Back on Life—There's no Time Like Now to Learn from Your Past

voice inside us said that there was a reason why he was in his specific situation. Even though our opinion of Jack was that he was not good enough for Jill, we respected her decision to try to share and build a life with him. Over time, we started to see signs of a toxic relationship. Later, we found out that he was physically abusive towards her, and yet she persevered in holding onto that relationship, wanting to make it work.

I hate to admit this, but while Jill was a beautiful young woman, hardworking and intelligent, with so much potential, Jack was garbage. He had plans to build a better future, however he had chosen a life of laziness and substance abuse in the past. Using the analogy of forks in the road, Jack always chose the easy road, even with opportunities presenting themselves.

As their relationship came to an inevitable end, they sold the house, made a profit, and gave us back the money we had given them. This is when my wife and I realized that we had just enabled Jack to go on living easily. Suddenly, he had $18,000 from the sale of their house, and we knew that it would all go into drinking and drugs. Meanwhile, Jill continued to try to straighten him out. I probably don't need to tell you this, but you can't change people. This will sound harsh, but you have to leave garbage in the garbage. Otherwise they will drag you down with them. Making a change is a personal decision. No one can make another person want to improve themselves or create a better life. While Jack was unemployed and spending his days drinking, Jill was working and planning to continue her education.

The life lesson for me was this: if you see a problem, call it out. It may not make you popular at the time. But by the time you're older, you'll have learned a lot, even though you may not have it all figured out. And it's your responsibility to point this out to other people. Of course, we all make our own mistakes in life. We learn from them. We pay the consequences.

There's a specific pattern I often see with new consultants, in which they tell me their problems, and with an attitude of putting the blame on others, they play the victim of their circumstances. All I can do in this situation is tell them the truth about what they need to do in order to succeed. Unfortunately, this type of person clings to their victim mentality and rejects everything I tell them. They perceive me as someone who is persecuting them for their situation, and in their eyes, I am the bad guy.

The hard truth is worth repeating: Nine times out of ten, people are in their situation for a reason. We—you and me—cannot save the world. We try. Of course we do. Our hearts are in the right place. We genuinely care about people. But the reality is that all we end up doing is frustrating ourselves.

Another lesson I've learned over the years, especially in this business, is that often individuals are so eager to build their respective business that they give their downline false expectations about how much money they will make and how quickly. Multi-level is a legit business model and not a get-rich-quick scheme. What these eager individuals should be passing on is what I call "the $500 story." I love this story because it's realistic and begins with a question:

What would an extra $500 a month mean to you?

If you had $500 net from your business on top of your day job, what would that mean? It could mean three things:

It could mean that you could take that $500 and put it into a college education fund for your kids. You may think $500 isn't a lot of money, but when you think about how much an education costs (typically between $30,000 and $50,000 a year), $500 a month becomes $6,000 in savings in one year. If your kid is 10 years old at

Principle 6: Look Back on Life—There's no Time Like Now to Learn from Your Past

the time, throw in the interest and dividends, and over the course of seven years you've just doubled your money. By the time your kid is 17 years old, what a great feeling it would be to hand over a check towards their education.

The other two things that $500 a month could mean are equally important. You could save toward your retirement or long-term care. These are facts of life. Our future years will require money. All that to say that we should be talking about real expectations rather than false expectations when building our respective teams. By sharing real expectations, your people will stick around because they have a better foundation of what they can expect and build with. This is a truism.

As well, no matter what you're striving for, you're not going to do it all today. As I get older, I realize that everything has to be one day at a time, one goal at a time. An example of a small goal in this business is the decision or commitment to speak to ten people a week. Out of those ten people, maybe one or two will consider joining your business and one or two will decide to buy products. This type of realistic and consistent expectation from yourself is solid math. Speaking to ten people a week leads to 40 people a month. That's 480 people a year. When you're talking to 480 people a year about anything, you're going to reach the right people.

As leaders, it's our responsibility to give people the right expectations as opposed to unrealistic ones like "we're going to make you $50,000 a month." I'm not trying to sell anyone a pipe dream. I'm trying to tell people what I've learned and how they can take it further. While I don't believe in get-rich-quick schemes, I do believe that you can become very wealthy by your own standards in network marketing over a period of time by doing things right, by being consistent, and by building a team with realistic expectations.

Another point I want to make about being realistic is that we all have a lot to deal with in terms of juggling the process of building a business, family issues, and whatever else comes into our lives. Yet we feel that we have to have this happy face on all the time. Even that's unrealistic. The truth of the matter is that it's okay to tell people that you have some other stuff going on and that you may not be able to call them for a couple of days.

They'll probably respect you for it, because when it's their turn, you're not sitting there expecting them to produce or they're not feeling guilty because they missed a conference call because they've had to deal with something. It's okay. Life goes on.

I've been in this business since 1983, and companies like Mary Kay, Herbalife, and Amway were all around even back then. They'll probably be here long after I'm gone. So, what's the rush?

While it's good to work fast and hard, it's more important to work consistently. Over the years, that's probably the most important lesson I've learned. And this doesn't just apply to this business model but to all businesses and all areas of life. Slow and steady is better than burning out.

Thoughts from Foster ...

We all have memories—some are good, some are bad. The important takeaway throughout our lives is to learn from the past and make the best of it going forward.

For me personally, the death of my parents at such a young age has prepared me in five specific areas:

1. Faith
2. Trust

3. Growth
4. Courage
5. Love

1. FAITH

What's important here is not faith in a spiritual sense, but rather in general. In other words, faith in things, faith in other people, faith in life, faith in situations. Whether we like it or not, the issue of faith arises in every area of business, and it is important to understand the meaning that it brings. I can say that I have faith in the project we're working on right now—the writing of this book, the one you hold in your hands. I have faith in our future. What is this faith based on? It's based on the past. The past, which always includes many setbacks.

Throughout the years I've been asked how I continued to hold on to future aspirations when at the very young age of seven, I lost my mother and saw it happen. That was my first experience with death. Then, just over seven years later my father passed away. This is where I learned that faith, by holding on to a better tomorrow, helps keep you going in the face of adversity. Looking back, I realize that faith is a very critical component. We all must have that faith to keep going.

A question that often comes up is, what is the difference between faith and hope? Faith is stronger than hope. For example, perhaps you walk through the bushes without wearing any shoes and you "hope" that you won't step on something sharp. I experienced this. I stepped on a piece of glass that cut my toe in two. I lived in a town where there was no hospital or ambulance or paramedics, no traditional medical care. If you were bleeding, all you could do was hold the skin very tight while trying to find something to stop the bleeding. And you survive without any real explanation as to why your life was spared.

I mention this not because it's sad, but because there are a lot of good things behind every situation. Today, I can see that there was a purpose for certain situations and happenstances, because here I am. I get to travel, and my story has enriched the lives of others by helping them realize that giving up is never an option.

2. TRUST

The kind of trust I'm referring to is more about trust in others in spite of the fact that at certain times in my life, especially during my childhood years, everything around me seemed so dim. The light at the end of the tunnel for me was one of those things where I had to trust others to lead me into the light, day by day, because who else did I have around me? My mom and dad were gone. I had no choice but to trust.

There are certain decisions I have been able to make consciously throughout my life. At the same time, there are also situations where I was forced to make decisions. Whether that's a job or a career choice, sometimes you just have to trust that whoever is helping you to put food on the table has your best interests at heart.

A good example of this was my very first job in Montreal, where I worked the night shift folding boxes at a plastic factory. It may not seem like much, but someone helped me to get that job so that I could start my life in a new country. I had to *trust* that the path I was on would lead me somewhere—lead me to something better. And that trust paid off.

3. GROWTH

Looking back on my life, I now see growth as equivalent to personal development. It is a lifelong process and a way for all of us to

Principle 6: Look Back on Life—There's no Time Like Now to Learn from Your Past

assess our individual skills and qualities to see if we can do something more than what we currently see before us. As I mentioned, my first job in Canada was working in a plastic factory. But with personal growth I had the opportunity to assess my own skills and qualities, and eventually I realized that I could do better. I could do more than what I was doing at the time. This brings me to the next topic.

4. COURAGE

Courage is something we must practice on a daily basis. The courage to not quit when our plan seems to be going off course. The courage to not give up on ourselves, even when life gets tough. And as we all know, life does get tough sometimes.

Even when you find something that you're passionate about, what I've learned from looking back is that it's still going to take courage to persevere. It's still going to take courage to stay consistent and to deal with the highs and the lows, because nobody stays on top all the time. A good example is winning an Olympic gold medal. It's very hard to maintain that level of performance for the remainder of your life. And it takes courage to also assess some of the fallbacks and to know that you can always pick yourself up. You don't have to be number one all the time to be successful. You'll always be in the game as long as you don't quit. That in itself takes courage.

You look at some of the problems that we face in life, and sometimes you simply have to let go and let God. There are certain days—even now—that I just cannot manage on my own. And as simple as letting go sounds, it's actually very hard. It's a very big step. Most of us like to approach life with a lot of optimism, but at the same time, there's nothing wrong with being cautious.

While some may see the fact that I grew up without running water and electricity as unfortunate, I see it in a different light. I feel fortunate to have grown up in a small village where no one ever had to worry about things like losing their home in a fire. I've also been very fortunate in that I've been mentored by a lot of great people, both directly and indirectly. People that inspired me and even blessed me with their knowledge. All these blessings are not just on me, but on others as well. My children are beneficiaries of this, as are my business associates.

This brings us to the topic of leadership. Again, looking back on my childhood years and the environment in which I was born, where we had only the essentials. Some may see this as having no value. But instead, I've chosen to grow a business and share my blessings with others. I take my role as a business leader very seriously. My goal is to always make a positive contribution.

Part of the reason for us wanting to write this book is that we want to share the message that leadership, whether it's by appointment or otherwise, is an opportunity and a privilege that should never be abused. As leaders, we have a responsibility that includes preparing future generations to be able to care for tomorrow in a meaningful way. This is true whether our leadership role is as parents or businesspeople.

5. LOVE

We have to look at all the topics we've just discussed—faith, trust, growth, and courage—with more inclusiveness than we have in the past. An inclusiveness that we have to continue to strive for. Using someone like Nelson Mandela as an example, it takes a special kind of love to be able to spend over 27 years in prison and then come back and take on the responsibility of being the leader of a country without being disillusioned.

Of course, there are areas in my life that sadden me and even people that have done me wrong. But when you strive to have love in your heart, you are able to somehow forgive, forget, and move on. This doesn't mean that the memory goes away. When I say "forget," it doesn't mean that you don't remember all the past hurts. But overall, in spite of some of the challenges and setbacks, I honestly believe that God has spared my life. I'm here to continue to share my blessings. It's important for me to look into the future with optimism. This is where leadership plays a critical role. It takes courage to have that balance and to make decisions that are not of a selfish nature. This all depends on how we want to grow as individuals in a fast-paced society.

CHAPTER 7

Principle 7: Observe the Financial Domino Effect

While the title of this chapter talks about the *financial* domino effect, the same principle can be applied to any area of life, whether the goal is to lose weight, improve your memory, or build a business. This is because everything begins with small steps that, when taken consistently, build momentum.

This is good news for anyone who feels overwhelmed by their ambitions. Yes, we all have big dreams. This is but ONE of the things that we, the writers of this book, and you, the reader, have in common. How do we know this? Because everything that we're sharing has been learned from personal experience, and the very fact that you're holding this book in your hands means that you have questions, perhaps even doubts. That said, we're confident that you'll feel a sense of relief after reading this chapter, and we encourage you to not only write down your goals (both financial goals and others), but also make a list of the tasks—or steps—that will lead you to achieving them.

Thoughts from John ...

The concept behind the *domino effect* is that one thing grows into another thing, which grows into something even better. It's all about building momentum. A good example comes from a number of years ago when I was consulting for a man whom we'll call David. David was an American, and his uncle was the founder of a major mail order company in the UK. Before founding his company, the uncle was a clockmaker who would take his clocks door to door in an effort to sell them. His challenge was that most people back then couldn't afford to buy a clock. As you can understand, this was a real problem for the clockmaker, because it was his source of income. If you can imagine, he was building an item that everyone needed yet could not afford.

This did not deter the clockmaker. Focused on finding a solution, he finally came up with one: a strategy that would benefit all involved. He came up with a plan whereby if his customers could come up with a down payment of one dollar, he could then get the bank to finance the balance of the cost of his clock. The bank would make money on the interest, his customers would get the clock they wanted, and he would get to earn a living. A win-win for all involved. This is a great example of the domino effect in which one simple idea led to another greater idea.

A more current example is Jeff Bezos, known as the founder of Amazon.com. From the beginning, Jeff was adamant about putting his money back into his business. So much so that his original desk was an old door. While Jeff started by selling books online, one thing led to another, and his business evolved to what is today a hub for selling products—not just his, but other people's as well. Today he is one of the richest men in the world, with a net worth of over $150 billion at the time of this writing.

McDonald's is another good example of evolving with the times and how the domino effect occurs. McDonald's was originally known for its hamburgers. By adding salads to the menu, it now also caters to today's more health-conscious society.

Principle 7: Observe the Financial Domino Effect

From a networking standpoint, opportunities begin with a contact. I originally met my friend Sid over 30 years ago. At the time, Sid was a downline in my company, and we maintained a friendship even though we eventually went our separate ways with the particular business we were in. Over the years we lost contact, but then we got re-acquainted and today we have multiple business interests together in different industries around the world. The domino effect here is clear: I knew Sid from one business, and while he eventually got out of the network marketing industry, he never got out of business. Although he's no longer in network marketing, our affiliation there is how we started out together.

Fundamentally, the domino effect is a growth principle. Going back to the McDonald's reference, J. R. Simplot was a potato farmer from Idaho who earned the deal of a lifetime when he figured out how to freeze-dry his potatoes and became the first supplier of French fries to McDonald's. From there, Mr. Simplot got involved in the computer processor industry when he became the investor who helped fund Micron.

All these examples teach the lesson that opportunities are everywhere, and you never know what a chance meeting or idea will lead to. One big mistake that people make is when they decide to cut the tie with someone simply because they're not interested in their business offering. Even though someone isn't interested in your network marketing business today, they could become a really good contact in the future for something completely unrelated. This is precisely why we help develop people and build relationships in this business.

Another great example begins with a woman named Mary Kay Ash, also known as the founder of the multimillion-dollar business, Mary Kay Cosmetics. Mary Kay basically started her company because she was the top salesperson at another company, and despite her achievements and success rate, she was passed over in 1961 for a senior-level sales position. She knew that she should have gotten the promotion. She'd worked hard and deserved it. This propelled her to start her own company in 1963. Not only did her action reflect her ability to stand up for herself, but for all women. By doing so, she turned a negative into a positive by transforming the gender-specific glass ceiling at the time into an infinite number of opportunities for women everywhere.

Thoughts from Foster …

The domino effect is something we can all relate to. We already know that the decisions we make—whether financial or not—have an impact. With or without the visual of falling dominoes, the domino effect is an important topic and reminder that our decisions have consequences. Add in the financial aspect, and the consequences from our choices hit home even harder. Some of us have a good relationship with our finances, but most of us do not.

When I look at the domino effect as it pertains to our business, you have one person succeed and they, in turn, teach someone else how to succeed. This idea of helping each other to achieve our own definitions of success continues to follow in the same domino effect.

Many years ago, I read *The Parable of the Pipeline* by Burke Hedges. To put this into context, I was raised in a small town where the only way to have water in your home was by carrying it home in buckets. The number of buckets that you carried would be equal to the amount of water that you had for the day. Some may take it for granted, but when you think about it, you need water for everything from cleaning to cooking to bathing. So, hauling water was a tedious job but a necessity for properly managing a family and household. The challenge in this scenario was that this task required you to be strong and healthy. In other words, if today you have a stiff neck or an aching back, you cannot carry a bucket. Yet you still need the water to survive. When I look back and compare that to today and the financial domino, I'm also looking at the way people live their lives in today's society. When I eventually left my village and made it to the city, I realized that everybody had pipelines that carried the water all the way from the river to their homes. If someone needed water, they could simply turn on the tap, and there it was. Once I got my head around this concept, what I loved about it was how efficient it is. Whether you're healthy, sick, or sleeping, water is always available thanks to the pipeline.

In contrast to this, a person with disabilities cannot carry a bucket. Or to bring this analogy closer to today's world, when you're an employee, you only get so many sick days and days off for vacation. Once those are used up, if—God forbid—you should get sick, you either no longer have an income or it's the end of your career. This is not something that I would wish on anyone, but I'm using it as an example to demonstrate the power of the financial domino principle and its ongoing effect.

In our line of work and business model, we continuously strive to enrich the lives of others; by doing so, you're indirectly enriching your own life. This, by definition, is the domino effect. Anyone that is doing very well with their own business is ultimately enriching the life of others, as demonstrated in the pipeline parable that tells the story of two young cousins living in a small village somewhere in Italy. Both bright and hardworking, the cousins had big dreams to one day become very rich. All they needed was an opportunity, which presented itself one day when the village elders decided to hire them to carry water from a nearby river to the town square. Their job was to bring in enough water for the entire town every day. At the end of each day, the cousins would get paid for the number of buckets they had carried to fill the village's cistern.

This was hard work, and inevitably the day came when one of the cousins was suffering from blistered feet from walking back and forth from the river as well as back pain from carrying bucket after bucket every day. This is when one of the cousins came up with a plan to build a pipeline from the river to the reservoir. Because this was a new idea for the time, everyone laughed at the cousin's plan. Regardless, he worked evenings and weekends on building his pipeline. Meanwhile, the other cousin was spending his free time at the bar, spending his hard-earned money on booze.

Six months down the road, there was real progress made by the cousin building the pipeline, and finally it was finished. He had built a pipeline that could easily run water straight from the river to the cistern. The analogy in this story that relates to the financial domino effect is that something that was taking all day (carrying water from the river to the village) was now being done by turning on a tap, and within minutes the cistern was full. Meanwhile, the cousin that laughed at the idea was no longer needed for his services because someone else had come up with a brilliant solution.

In today's economy, there's no real job security. At some point, an employer will no longer have use for your services, and you'll be replaced with a more efficient method for getting your work done. But if you create a system that can continue with an ongoing effect, you can create your own financial domino, and the effect of that can be very positive. This is where network marketing comes in. You do

Principle 7: Observe the Financial Domino Effect

the work today, which is today's sacrifice, and that's what is going to reward you tomorrow. Short-term pain equals long-term gain.

In other words, tomorrow's dreams are built on today's sacrifices. If a person can keep their eyes on the prize, they get to see how powerful this principle is. The financial domino effect is a concept that demonstrates how everything that we do has an effect. This can be a positive just as easily as it can be a negative. I like to focus on the fact that you can create something today that will continue to create an income even when you're no longer here.

CHAPTER 8

Principle 8: Watering the Seed

Discipline. Focus. Routine. Momentum. When it comes to achieving goals, these four words define the tools that will take you from where you are to where you want to be. In other words, from a desire or vision to the intended outcome or results. This applies to everything from attaining your ideal weight to living the lifestyle of your dreams. In sum, these four words can be defined by the age-old adage: *watering the seed.*

When you water a seed, you give it the care it needs to grow. You provide it with the right soil or environment for good results. And while this sounds like it applies to an outward goal such as business success or an achievement such as losing weight, it's actually an inside job. Attaining success, no matter what that means to you, begins with yourself in terms of self-development. This applies to growth, while giving you something to build on so that you can create the right mindset for the discipline, focus, routine, and momentum required for achieving your goals.

For the seed, we talk about the right amount of water, sunlight, and good soil for growth. For you, this translates into a healthy environment and positive mindset.

When you break these four words down—discipline, focus, routine, and momentum—they are *actionable*. This puts you in a great position because it means that you have control over whether or not you will succeed or accomplish your goal.

You develop discipline.
You direct your focus.
You stick to a routine.
You build momentum.

A great way to demonstrate the power of these four tools is to think about the opposite: *neglecting the seed*. Poor soil and lack of water can only yield the opposite of success; namely, no growth and no activity at all.

Again, this also applies to your goals and self-development. Surround yourself with people that don't inspire you, that "bring you down," and neglect to take consistent action toward your goals and you'll remain where you are today: wishing, hoping, dreaming.

Oddly, the opposite of these four action words is one simple nonaction word: neglect. As we know, it's easier to do nothing. But put consistent effort into achieving your goals, and magic happens as your dreams grow into your reality.

Thoughts from John ...

One of my many mentors in both business and life was the late Jim Rohn. Known as an entrepreneur, author, and motivational speaker, one of the things he used to say was, *"All distractions are equal."*

What he meant by that is that a distraction can be anything—even simply watching a sports game when you know you should be planning for your next conference call. Don't get me wrong. I'm a sports fan too and love a good game. After all, balance between spending time building a business and personal interests is important. But in today's world, that's not a viable excuse, because you can record things; there's no reason to miss anything. Even good excuses are no longer excuses.

What happens is, everything in life leads to habits, and people create bad habits. Not to say that you shouldn't enjoy your life and watch a game once in a while, but there are so many of these distractions. The point is that whether it's a game or your favorite cooking show, all these distractions are equal, and if they distract you from your business, they're going to interrupt the process of building momentum and moving forward. More importantly, these distractions create bad habits, and once you create them, they're very hard to get rid of. It's even comparable to an addiction.

I truly believe that the direct selling industry is a self-development business with a marketing plan. It's a way for you to get paid for your own growth. And the more skills you acquire, the less you get distracted. As you progress in the business through the years, you will find that you'll get less and less distracted. You can get more done in four focused hours today than ever before, thanks to technology and the many tools we have access to.

I've seen it happen time and time again. For example, years ago when I was living in New Jersey, I had a consultant on my team who was a schoolteacher. He initially did very well in the business on a part-time basis. At the time he had young children and was what I would consider a very focused person. When he worked part-time on his business, he found a way to build it despite everything else going on in his life, including his family, his full-time job, and his involvement with his church. He got to the point where he was averaging $5,000 to $6,000 a month within about 90 days of starting his business. He was a very likeable person. The type of person that walks into a room and everyone gravitates towards him.

With his rapid success, he decided that he wanted to focus on his business on a full-time basis, and I remember cautioning him about that. I thought he was making a mistake. Even though he had already proven that he had a strong sense of discipline, his full-time teaching job provided him with security, benefits, and time off during the holidays and summer months. But he thought that by focusing on one thing only—his business—he would have more time to spend with his kids during the day.

Finally, he took the plunge and left his job with the school to build his business. Within less than three months he went from making $5,000 a month to making $2,000 a month. He basically blew himself out of the business because he was no longer meeting people organically as he had before with his teaching job. Not only that, but he was so distracted by all his free time (taking his kids to the park, etc.) that he destroyed his own business. As it turned out (and this happens often), all the extra time that he no longer had to dedicate to his teaching job wasn't applied to his business. He ended up losing the discipline that had made him so successful in the first place.

I'm going to share a story that is the flip side to that. This story is also about a schoolteacher. During this second person's first two years in the business with me, he continued to teach school. He actually got to the point where he started to double his income with his part-time MLM business before he decided to quit his teaching job and go full-time with his business.

Another case is that of a financial planner I know who lives in Idaho. He and his wife built their business into a very nice organization. They were making over $15,000 a month and never gave up their financial planning practice. With the contacts that they made from their "day job," they saw the bridge between their two businesses and how both represented opportunities for cross-over business. Once again this demonstrates that if you're not distracted, you can handle multiple businesses, and even multiple ventures with your time as long as you stay disciplined.

One of the biggest mistakes that people make is to glorify the freedom. They think that because they're "in business for themselves," they're entitled. A good way to demonstrate this is by imagining that you buy a McDonald's restaurant. I like to use McDonald's as a reference because it's a proven business model and has a strong brand. So, you buy into a McDonald's restaurant, which makes you self-employed. All is well, except that one morning you go into work and you find out that the truck that was supposed to deliver the eggs for all the breakfasts you know you'll be serving didn't show up. Maybe it had a flat tire or maybe it got into an accident. That's not the point. The point is that things like that do happen. So, what do you do? How do you react?

Most people see themselves as "the boss." They've made this big investment and are therefore entitled to an income. But that's not the right answer. What you really need to do is get your butt in the car and go down to the 7/11 or wherever you can find the eggs that you need for your morning crowd. Otherwise you're not going to have a breakfast clientele and you're going to lose a lot of money that day and for days afterward, because word of mouth travels fast and people will hear that "the McDonald's wasn't serving eggs." Taking the action of going to find eggs is called self-responsibility.

The point here is that with freedom comes a lot of responsibility when you're self-employed. The people who understand this are the ones that are going to succeed. If they don't understand this, it can be very self-destructive, because instead of focusing on making their business work, they're busy taking that freedom for granted.

Certain aspects of my business are on my mind all the time, even when I'm on vacation. I may drive my wife and kids crazy with that, but we all like the lifestyle that I've been able to provide by keeping my eye on the ball and focusing on my business. I take the freedom as a blessing, but I also take it as a responsibility. I have to perform each and every day, even if it's for as little as an hour. I do what I have to in order to keep the momentum going for my organization and business. I have a responsibility to myself, but also to my team of consultants.

Granted, staying motivated every day is not easy. And that's precisely the reason why your "why" is so important. I've always been goal-oriented, and my original "why" was to have enough money put away so that by the time I reached the age of 50, working would be an option. That vision of having the freedom to do what I wanted later in life is what kept me motivated. Whether your goal is long-term or you choose to envision short-term goals such as a vacation, you need to write it down. Your "why" is what's going to remind you of what you need to do and motivate you to get it done.

Most people consider money as their "why," and if that's the case, you have to ask yourself an important question: For what? To get clear, you have to answer that "what" question. Is it a thing? A charity? A trip? An amount of money that you know you need in order to retire? You need to answer that question for yourself. If you don't have an answer, you have no direction.

I had a very simple goal when I started in the networking marketing industry: I wanted to earn $1 million. There's a difference between earning a million dollars and being a millionaire. I knew that and had the goal to earn it for the first time by the time I reached 30 years of age. And because of my competitive nature—as an athlete and in everything else that I do—I achieved it.

William O'Neil, the former publisher and editor for the business-focused paper *Investor's Business Daily*, had a great statement: *How you think is everything.* How we think about our business determines its outcome. Sometimes we get distracted by anything from the weather to world events. With the exception of 9/11 and the death of my own father and the death of our daughter, throughout the more than 37 years of my business career, I haven't taken more than three consecutive days off. Am I crazy? Probably. But I chose this, and the results speak for themselves.

One piece of advice that I often share is to spend 15 minutes a day on self-development, whether that's reading the Bible or listening to a motivational speaker. What's 15 minutes out of a 24-hour day? This helps make you a more well-rounded person. It's about consistently watering the seed, which in this context is your business and yourself. Just remember that good soil (in this context, your mind) will yield good results. As well, surrounding yourself with good people creates a good environment.

Thoughts from Foster ...

Watering the seed is a principle that I believe fits in with our responsibilities. When I look at this from the viewpoint of being a parent, I like to make the connection with our responsibilities. For example, initially it is our responsibility to know that our children are not going to be able to tie their own shoelaces. Our job as parents is mentoring, and part of that is making sure that our children are well groomed and well guided.

One question that comes up often is, "How long will I need to be there for them?" Whether we're referring to our responsibilities as parents or as business mentors, the answer to that question is however long it takes. No one has a set timetable that determines the number of weeks, months, or years that a child or colleague will need us for. When it comes to watering the seed, it's more of a healthy environment that you are creating.

Let's look at it from a farming point of view: You have to plant a seed, but if you don't protect that seed, at some point, weeds will get in the way and probably choke it out so that it doesn't have a chance to grow. So, you water it. You make sure that the seed has a clear path and clean environment to grow into a healthy plant. You cannot just plant a seed and sit back and fold your arms and expect great things to happen.

Using our line of business as an example, I always say that it's easy to sign somebody up into your network marketing business. The real work begins on the day that you look the person straight in the eyes and say, "We're going to succeed together." That's the commitment that you make to that person. It's a promise and marker of your integrity. Succeeding together cannot be something like throwing mud on the wall, hoping that it's going to stick. You have to nurture that process by making sure that whatever mud you throw on the wall is going to be well plastered. You have to ensure that you're going to give it the TLC that it needs to stick.

Part of watering the seed is looking at the unique skills and talents that people bring to the table. There are certain things that we call potential: A positive attitude. A level of commitment. A person's enthusiasm. All the things that I call the 97% and that make me say, "Okay, this person has the potential to succeed." The remaining 3% is what I call the "skills." The skills comprise what it takes to get a person involved and in center field.

You can be motivated and committed, but if you don't have the skills, that 3%, this can impact whether you succeed or fail. This is why we need teachers and coaches, to make sure that people have access to learn the right skills in order to be able to do what they need to succeed. A person may be motivated and even committed to spending all their days in a mall trying to hand out flyers. But if they don't know how to have a conversation with a person and ask the right questions, they're not going to get the results they want. This is all part of the learning curve.

We are in the business of people, where getting appointments for conference calls and face-to-face meetings is essential. It's been proven that if you can get ten out of every ten appointments with every contact you make, your business is going to soar. We also know that if you can get five out of ten people to meet with you, you're going to do very well. But it takes skills to be able to get five or more appointments out of the ten calls you make.

I've seen situations where a person didn't have the right skills, so they asked the wrong questions and didn't get the results they wanted. If you and I are co-workers and during our coffee break I ask you what you do for a living, this is obviously the wrong question, because we work together. I should know what you do for a living. If I want to tell you about my business and the opportunity it presents, it takes skill to know the right questions to ask. The right question may be, "What do you do during your free time?" Or asking about holidays and vacations. Then, based on their answers, I can ask a follow-up question.

A good example is someone who says they like to go fishing. A follow-up question could be how often they get to go fishing. They may respond by saying that they don't go as often as they'd like because of work. From there I can talk about establishing a business that would provide them with more free time. The skill is to be able to ask the right questions, which lead to the right follow-up questions. At the same time, it helps you to understand what's important to that person. This all comes with experience and the right guidance.

Where many people fail is that they bring someone into the business and then they leave them hanging because they're moving on to the next person without really watering that seed. A long-term benefit for all associates is to be able to spend time with their people and help them to succeed. It's a lot of work to be constantly looking for new recruits if you can't help the ones you bring in. This isn't working smart. On the other hand, I know people in this industry who work smart for three weeks and then take one week off every single month. These people literally take twelve vacations a year.

As mentioned earlier, there's no specific timetable for how long you have to work with an individual. The most important thing is to look for people with a strong desire to succeed and to nurture them. The title of "mentor" or "leader" is not something to be taken lightly. When you tell someone you're going to help them succeed, this is something that you should take seriously. It truly is a responsibility.

CHAPTER 9

Principle 9: Showing Love for Others

While you might not expect a chapter on *showing love for others* in a business book, this is actually one of the most powerful tenets of the network marketing industry, one that separates it from other business models. Although in existence since the 1920s, at some point direct selling acquired a negative stigma, not unlike that of the "used car salesman" from the 1960s. This is both unfortunate and wrong.

As discussed in an earlier chapter, a unique and powerful aspect of this industry is that it encourages self-development. Some of the most recognized thought leaders in network marketing acknowledge that attaining success—no matter what that means to you—can only be achieved by growing as a person and genuinely caring about others.

And so, without further ado, it is our pleasure to share our thoughts and experiences on this topic with you.

Thoughts from John ...

I firmly believe that the most important way that we can help others is by setting a good example for them. By taking responsibility for ourselves, including self-care and taking care of our families, we teach others how to do the same. Especially in a capitalist society, by helping the people that we care for to attain the skills they need, we encourage them to become self-reliant.

Ronald Reagan is known to have said that of all the "isms," capitalism is the best even with its many flaws. As a capitalist and an entrepreneur, as a businessperson and a sales leader, whatever you want to call yourself, one of the most important things you can do is lead by example. By doing so, you're helping the greater good.

What do I mean by "the greater good"? The greater good is this: If you're successful, in theory you pay more in income tax. And you certainly consume more items, which contributes to the economy, whether it's the local economy or the global economy. Once again, how do you show love for others? You do that by getting personal, to the point where you need more of what they have to offer (whatever that happens to be in terms of goods and services in your community) and you pay more taxes; you're helping to build Little League fields and better hospitals and better schools and better fitness centers and parks for the community at large.

I once gave a speech on capitalism, and someone challenged me on it afterward. I responded by saying that I have yet to see a socialist or communist build anything sustainable, long-term. Yet when I look at people like Bill Gates or Michael Dell or Steve Jobs or Henry Ford ... all these people have built sustainable models that employed tens of thousands of people for decades and longer. At the end of the day, they profit and become wealthy. But more importantly, they accomplish something by serving the greater good. Their efforts help build stronger communities.

Self-love and loving your neighbor are really the same thing. If you don't love yourself, you cannot love the guy next door. It's impossible, because it's an emotional inconsistency. If I don't love myself and I think of myself as worthless, it's really hard to go out there and tell other people that they should attain greatness in whatever they're doing. My point here is that everything—EVERYTHING—begins with self-love.

Over 30 years ago I was quoted as saying, "To love people, you use money." I still believe that to this day. Money is to serve the greater good, whether that's toward charity or your church or putting your kids through school. You make money so that you can spread it around.

Here's another example: when I look at my current product, which is the core product that we sell through our respective network marketing businesses, I think about how that product started with farmers in Idaho taking care of and maintaining their cattle. Using a family farm as an example, there's a farmer who gets paid to take care of that herd, and he sells X number of gallons every year to make the product. Does he help his community in Idaho by paying taxes that sustain the hospitals and Little League field? Of course he does.

Then there's me. I strive every day to build a bigger business by creating more demand. Now that farmer needs more cows, and perhaps more farmers are required to fill that demand. My business trickles down to helping the family farmer and others. Then take that a step further. Obviously that milk needs to get from Idaho up to Montreal, where the product is manufactured. Well, that means that there's a truck involved, which means that there's a trucking company involved, which means that there are dispatchers involved, and mechanics involved to maintain those vehicles. Now once again, are all these people involved getting paid to do what they do? Yes, they are. And again, by building my business I've created a second set of jobs with the need to transport the product.

Then once the product gets to Montreal, there are people working in the manufacturing facilities. Then for the packaging, there's a packaging company that employs people that once again pay taxes in their community, and that grows their respective community. The bigger I build my business, the more jobs I create. The more jobs I create, the more love I'm showing, as these people get to take care of themselves and their families. This point is important: to be an entrepreneur who creates jobs is a noble thing.

Somehow a stigma has been created that by building a business I'm taking advantage of people. But it's really the opposite. I love what I'm doing. I love hearing that someone is becoming a billionaire, because by them becoming a billionaire, they've created a lot of millionaires that have created a lot of sub-millionaires. All because they've created a lot of jobs. Meanwhile, people are paying their taxes. They're taking care of their loved ones. They're sending their kids to decent schools. So, by being an entrepreneur, I've actually done a good thing. This is a noble profession and possibly even the most noble of professions.

All that said, it certainly helps you when you get skilled at what you do. And by getting skilled at what you do, you in turn bless a whole lot of other people, not just your family. This business model and industry is very people-oriented. As mentioned, it encourages both the development of skills and the development of self.

Thoughts from Foster ...

Show love for others. This topic is very dear to my heart, as I believe that life is all about love. In a world filled with contrast, you either love or you hate. Showing love toward another is a decision. It's the right decision, no matter what the circumstances are. And it is my belief that we all want to make the right decision. I don't know anyone that chooses to hate without having to face consequences. Especially since love is something that we all desire.

One thing about love that I know for sure is that when you help to carry each other's burdens, it makes every weight lighter. When you are carrying each other's burdens, even if you don't think about what you're going to get in return, there's always a reward because you're doing it with love. There are several quotes that we've shared with our networks, and one in particular, which we actually live, talks about when you help enough people get what they want, you will always get everything you want. This philosophy is more powerful than people realize.

Even if you're dealing with someone that does not understand love, when you are loving with all your heart, it is impossible not to receive love in return. To use a personal experience as an example, when my wife and I were first dating, I laid everything on the table. I did not hold back. And that set me free. To this day, I don't ever have to worry about her finding out about something, because what you see is what you get. This is me. Instead of feeling ashamed, I shared my past and my struggles from a place of love. For example, up until I was 15 years old, I slept on a mat and knew nothing about comfortable mattresses. For me to be able to really be open with my wife was one way for me to express my love and my gratitude. That brought us very close, and she was able to open up to me in return. We come from completely different backgrounds, so this was important to both of us as well as important for our relationship. I truly believe that there are so many ways that you can show love toward another person. A small yet very significant example is warming up her car in the morning. This seems trivial, but it means so much to her. In return, she naturally does things for me without her even having to try to make me happy.

Looking at our business model in particular, helping others or doing things to help someone succeed organically creates security for you. In our line of work, I always say that my goodness does not show down, it shows up. And guess who is up there: everyone that has helped me. It's an indirect way of giving back. When we can show love to others without worrying about what we're going to gain in return, it helps us to go all out, and frankly, love has no limits.

I find that when you love, it takes an enormous burden off your shoulders. But when you hate, it's almost like you're constantly having to watch your back, and even having to explain why you're doing certain things. When you're showing love, you'll rarely be asked, "Why are you being so nice?" But when you are mean to others and have a hateful attitude, it makes people question everything about you. This is because it's not the natural thing that people expect from others. When a person has caused a lot of pain, even after they've been forgiven, there are still scars that remain in the hearts of others. Hate is never a good thing. The opposite is true with love. When you show love, you leave a permanent imprint of goodness.

A few years ago, I received news that my all-time mentor, Richard DeVos, the founder of the Amway Corporation, passed away. About 30 years ago this man tapped me on the shoulder and said, "Son, you have the right posture. You keep doing what you're doing, and you will become successful one day." Now that is love. That is somebody speaking love. Thirty years later, I still hear his voice. I still feel his hand on my shoulder. This is what I call "a lasting impact."

Love can be demonstrated in so many ways. This is a man that I didn't know until I was introduced to network marketing. And because of his love for the industry and his love for mankind, he touched the lives of millions of people. Love has a way of doing wonders. When you show love for others, it will have a positive, lasting impact.

We parents know this. We love our children. And if you can love other children in the same way that you love your own child, or love other people the same way that you love yourself, it will affect the world that we live in. Showing kindness and a sincere interest in someone else's success is a beautiful thing, and it is contagious.

There's a young fellow that lives in the Dominican Republic who recently became the first Platinum Consultant in his country for the company he represents. This young man, who was only 15 years old when he first came to listen to a conference, has achieved something great for himself and for those around him. He is remarkable. And when you watch him work, you really see this. His discipline and dedication are amazing.

Again, showing love for others can be just our own sense of gratitude. I'm looking at this young man and he has every reason to show gratitude toward his sponsor, because if that person had not shared the business opportunity with him, who knows where he would be today.

I believe there are no conditions to love. Learning how to love may be difficult for some people, but I don't think love is something that should have conditions. It should be unconditional and without judgment. I look at our business, and some people may come in and they're good to go from day one. With other people it's different. You have to find ways to run with those that can run, jog with those that can jog, crawl with those that can crawl. And sometimes just stop and ask, "Do you need a hand?" And look behind you to see who is reaching for that hand.

Sometimes it's just that little touch. And I believe that this business gives you the opportunity to do that. We can see people for their strengths and their weaknesses because we are all different. My wonderful city of Toronto is multi-cultural, and I always say that it is multi-complex because everybody is different. Because of love for one another and love for each other, we're able to live peacefully. With love we can achieve anything. There's no way that we can do anything great without having love behind it. I like to say that love is the foundation for all great things to happen. Love is also the pillar that holds everything in place.

CHAPTER 10

Principle 10: Train yourself to Think the Way that Successful People Think

Training ourselves to have the right mindset is a very important step toward success. We all know that successful people—those that have achieved great things regardless of circumstances and challenges—have an extraordinary way of thinking.

The question is, *how do they think?* And more importantly, *how did they learn to think that way?*

As we often say, success leaves clues. This chapter reveals some important insights into the way that ordinary people—people just like us—have managed to accomplish some pretty extraordinary feats. Our hope is that these revelations will give you the guidance required for turning your dreams into your ideal life.

Thoughts from John ...

It seems obvious, but it's worth stating: Successful people think and do what unsuccessful people are not willing to think and do. The difference between these two sets of people is that successful people are more proactive. Here's an example of how a typical person generally thinks, "I want to bench-press 500 pounds, but I don't want to go to the gym today. I'll think about it ... watch a movie about it. ... I'll go to the gym tomorrow."

The bottom line is that most people do not take the actions that are required for them to achieve their goals. And most importantly, they don't CONSISTENTLY do what it takes to achieve their goals. Generally, the people who succeed are the ones that are consistently proactive. They have meetings. They have conference calls. They have individual calls. They're constantly talking to people, be it on social media or face-to-face. In our business specifically, people that are successful are constantly chatting with at least ten people per day about their opportunity.

It's also worth noting that when you're proactive, you will make more mistakes than the inactive person. And that's a good thing, because we learn a lot from failure; perhaps even more than we learn from success. In other words, you can't fail just because you're thinking about something. Not doing anything because you're listening to your fear may seem like the safer path, but it's not. On the positive side, when you try and fail, you get to figure out why something didn't work—this time!

Two great quotes from Edison are, *"I have not failed. I've just found 10,000 ways that won't work."* And, *"Many of life's failures are people who did not realize how close they were to success when they gave up."*

I love these quotes because they show "failure" from the perspective of a renowned genius. The difference between success and failure is mindset, but it's also taking the actions required to see that doing something one way may seem to work, but if you tweak it, even just a little, the next time it may work even better. Taking action and being open to learn are things that set successful people apart.

Really, what it comes down to is that the difference between being successful or not is that you have to be willing to not only try but try continuously while constantly tweaking. Second, I think you have to study what success is and how it pertains to you. For example, I won't spend a lot of time watching true crime shows because I don't intend to kill anyone. On the other hand, if there's a documentary or biography about someone I admire for their accomplishments or tenacity, such as Steve Jobs, Bill Gates, Warren Buffett, Henry Ford, or an athlete or musician, then I'm all ears.

A good example of studying success is taking someone like Henry Ford and looking at what he did to build the Ford Motor Company—from paying people enough that they could actually buy the cars that they were making to developing the conveyor belt. Technology back then was to give people a specific job. Rather than having ten guys each doing ten different things slowly, let each guy do one thing and become an expert at it.

A concept that Ford came up with is "make enough cars and have the right price point so that people can actually afford them." He was years ahead of his time in terms of technology. But who did Ford spend his time talking to? He spent his time talking to people like George Washington Carver, a great inventor in his own right. As well, Ford befriended Thomas Edison. We can only imagine what those conversations must have been like.

I can't stress this enough: if you want to be successful, you study success. If you want to make a lot of money, you study people that make a lot of money. So basically, you fill your mind with the right information and thoughts and focus on what you want to achieve. In the same vein, if you're going to be successful, you need to associate yourself with successful people.

If you surround yourself with people that are on the right track in life, you're generally going to stay on the right track too. One of the reasons that I hang out with Foster is that Foster is a very positive person. No matter what the circumstances, he always looks at the bright side. Admittedly, I don't always look at the bright side of things.

But Foster … he's always looking at "I have this great life and this great wife and these great kids and this great house and I live in a great country …" and he looks at everything from that standpoint. He feels blessed because he is blessed. It could also be said that Foster is blessed because he feels blessed. This is a quality that I admire in him.

I believe that associating with people that are on the right track, people that want to do something with their lives, and people who always look on the bright side of things is how you train your mind for success. Once again, we go back to history and Dr. Norman Vincent Peale and the whole idea of positive thinking. This is something that I grew up with. The first book I ever read on self-development was *The Power of Positive Thinking*. The concepts in that book are all success concepts, and I adopted many of them into my daily living and thinking.

Putting yourself in the right mindset includes surrounding yourself with the right people, watching the right shows, listening to the right podcasts, and reading the right books, articles, and even blogs.

I'm always asking myself, "How can I do more and how can I learn more?"—Not just for my business but for my life. Another great quote is, "How you think is everything." At the end of the day, that says it all. If you're negative and you don't think anything you do will ever work, well, you're probably going to be right. On the other hand, if you think, "I don't have this figured out right now, but I will figure it out," eventually you will figure it out. Whether you think you can or think you can't, you're right.

Thoughts from Foster …

Successful people definitely think differently. While we talk about mindset, it's safe to say that successful people tend to think big.

Principle 10: Train yourself to Think the Way that Successful People Think

To remind myself of that, the license plate on my car says, "dream big." What does that mean? To help break it down, let's say that you work for a company as the cleaning person. The way I see it is that even though at that time you're only there as the person who cleans, you can still think like the CEO, regardless of your title or position. If you look at yourself as "just a cleaner," then you'll always think that you're just a cleaner. It's an attitude.

I look at everything that I've done to this point, and if there's one thing that I've done right, it has been to always keep the right attitude. I believe that this is how my brain is wired, and I'm grateful, because when I look at where I came from and where I am today, I realize that this is a powerful tool.

If a person can actually think like a CEO, regardless of the title they have, they can actually become a CEO, because there's not a single person who is a CEO today that did not start somewhere. Again, it's an attitude. It's a way of thinking without limits. It's about having a vision.

Even when a successful person has limitations, they don't see them as having any bearing on the outcome of their efforts. People who achieve success don't put limitations on themselves. In fact, we all know or have heard about someone that has overcome the odds, whether they're physical challenges or circumstantial. Their drive comes from an ability to look beyond whatever challenge they face and focus on their desired result. And you can train yourself to think this way. It begins as a habit, where you constantly and mindfully remind yourself to focus your thoughts and actions toward your goal. Eventually this habit turns into an attitude, also referred to as a mindset.

Successful people tend to have clear visions or clear goals of where they want to go, who they want to be, and what they want to achieve. I believe this is key. A good analogy to demonstrate this is a car. Someone can have the best car on the market, but if the driver doesn't know where they're going, it's just a nice car. One of the reasons why so many people are living in what I call developed countries yet still find themselves stuck is that they don't have a clear direction. You may be blessed, but if you have no idea how to cherish those blessings, it doesn't help you get further.

Passion is another important element in a person's ability to achieve success. Successful people tend to have passion for everything that they do. This passion becomes fuel for everything, and it drives them. If you have nothing running through you, sooner or later, you just give up. And then there are all the infamous excuses that we make. Successful people don't make excuses. Some people don't even allow age to get in the way of them achieving their goals.

Making sacrifices is something that most people are not willing to do. The truth is that if you want to be the best athlete or the best bodybuilder, you are going to have to make some serious sacrifices. There are things that you're going to have to give up and there are times when you're going to have to forgo doing things you enjoy. It really does take a willingness to make sacrifices to achieve your goals. In the long run, these sacrifices are small compared to the results.

Unfortunately, many people look at someone who has achieved success, and the first thing they think is that they were lucky. That's simply not true. It's the devotion that no one sees that is often misinterpreted as luck. This goes hand-in-hand with hard work.

No matter who you are—from Tiger Woods to Michael Jordan to Michael Jackson—any name that represents success is successful because the person worked hard. They may not work the typical nine to five, but they do work hard at their skills. Even what many

Principle 10: Train yourself to Think the Way that Successful People Think

of us interpret as "talent" is developed. While we may be born with specific inclinations (a love of sports or music, for example), if you don't work at developing them, they remain dormant within you.

Another important point is that successful people believe in themselves. They have a relentless belief that if someone has achieved it, they can too. They don't look at the obstacles; they look at the results or the achievement itself. They have faith. Even when they feel stuck, they have faith that they'll get through it. They have unshakable belief, unshakable faith, and hope. Because they're human, they will make mistakes along the way, but as mentioned earlier, mistakes are what bring us closer to breakthroughs.

This brings me to character. Successful people have character. And that character often includes integrity. You can be successful in something, but if you have no integrity, the success won't last.

Consistency is something that John mentioned, and I'd like to touch on it as well. Successful people don't have the bad habit that a lot of people have, which is to say to themselves, "Oh, I'll do it when I feel like it." If they decide to do something, they stick to it whether they feel like it or not.

CHAPTER 11

Principle 11: Build a Better Future–Starting Today

Building a better future is a universal topic that reflects every area of our lives, from our health to our finances. The good news is that whether we're in our 20s or our 50s, it's never too late to start thinking about ways to build a better life—a better life for today and tomorrow, because the future is as far as you plan and as close as the next sunrise. All you need to do is make a decision and take the right actions, with commitment and consistency. As you'll read in the following pages, building a better future begins today. It begins right now in this very moment and includes replacing old, hindering habits with new ones.

One of the great things about the way we've planned this book with shared thoughts from two individuals on separate yet joint journeys to success is that you, the reader, get to benefit from multiple points of view. In the cases of John and Foster, John focuses more on the financial aspects of building a better future. Foster reflects more on the importance of investing in yourself. We're confident that you'll find value in both.

Thoughts from John ...

As mentioned in the introduction to this chapter, it's never too late to start. That said, from a financial standpoint, the earlier you start to save money in life, the better off you'll be, because you will end up accumulating more. This is true whether you're contributing to your children's education fund or planning your own retirement. The way I see it, there are four basic needs for money:

1. Your children's education
2. Your personal retirement
3. Your own long-term healthcare
4. The long-term healthcare of a loved one

The last two in this list, your own long-term healthcare and the long-term healthcare of a loved one, are especially important since many people today live well into their 90s. Regardless of your lifestyle, you have to consider that it takes money to live and that the money you need, even just for basic necessities, has to come from somewhere. That said, let's say you're reading this and you're 50 years old and you don't have any savings. The truth of the matter is that while 50 to 70 may seem like a long time, the years fly by, and you're no longer in your prime working years.

Does this mean that it's too late to start? The answer to that is a definite NO. But it does mean that you need a practical and realistic approach to saving money. You need to be very disciplined with your money. This may rub some people the wrong way, but I'm not here to avoid hurting people's feelings. I'm here to share the information you need for building a better financial future. Truth be told, you simply can't save money while spending $8 every day on coffee from a coffee shop when you can make it at home for a fraction of the price.

Going through the drive-thru on your way to the office in the morning may not sound like a big deal when you're doing it today, but at the end of the week that $8 coffee turns into $45. At the end of the month, you've spent close to $200 on *coffee*.

If you take that same money and put it into a savings account (and there are many to choose from), over time you can accumulate more money with dividends and interest, depending on where you place it. At the end of the year, you're left with several thousand dollars that you can save without REALLY having tried. All you did was make your coffee at home instead of buying it from a coffee shop. Compound that small decision over ten years and that $8 a day has grown into tens of thousands of dollars in your bank account. That's a nice little nest egg.

I'm just using coffee as an example here, but in general, we don't realize the amount of money that we throw away on a regular basis. Another example of throwing away money while impacting our health in a negative way is buying and smoking cigarettes. Again, I'm not here to gently walk on eggshells. If you know me in person, you know that I like to call a spade a spade. Especially when it comes to making a point. And just the fact that you're reading this book tells me that you appreciate that.

The point with cigarettes and habits is that whether it's something bad for you or not, if you can live without it, you need to make the decision to do just that—live without it. Putting money aside is a discipline, and it may not feel like a lot when it's $10 or $20, but it adds up very, very quickly. That's not to say that you have to deprive yourself. Buying yourself a cup of coffee once in a while is great. Treating yourself and being kind to yourself is truly a gift, and from some perspectives, can even be seen as a privilege. But you need to realize the loss you're causing yourself when habits become daily treats because of the compound interest factor.

A good exercise is to make a list of all the things that you regularly spend money on. Then go through each and every item on that list and answer the question, *"Can I live without this?"* If the answer is yes, then you can take it from a daily purchase to a weekly or monthly "treat."

Another great and common example of waste falls under the category of time. How do you spend your time? Watching television is a great example of how many people spend—and waste—many hours of their time. Again, this isn't something that you need to cut out completely, but if you find that you're spending every evening binge-watching Netflix while wondering why you haven't written that book or learned how to play an instrument, or whatever goals you have for yourself, the answer is in how you're spending your time.

Listing the different ways that you regularly spend your time, from watching television to playing video games, and asking the same question (*"Can I live without this?"*) will help you determine what you can cut down on so that you can spend some of that time on activities that will help you gain momentum with the achievements that are important to you.

Trust me when I say that we're all guilty of this. Using an example from my own life, my health club costs me $80 a month. I use the free weights once a week, and the rest of the time that I'm there, I use the treadmill. Meanwhile, I actually own a treadmill. Right now, it's in my garage and it's being used as a place to store boxes. So, realistically I'm paying $80 a month to use a treadmill that I have sitting in my garage.

Comparison shopping is another factor to consider in our roles as consumers. From cars to homes to even the little items that seem insignificant but that compounded over time are very significant. As a society, we don't realize the little things that we can eliminate, cut down on, or purchase at a lower price. It goes without saying that some of our indulgences, including fast food or alcohol, are not good for our health. Limiting ourselves will improve our overall sense of well-being and give us more energy to do the things that are actually important. The bonus benefit is that creating new habits and approaching them with a sense of awareness will also be better for our bank accounts.

Is it too late to start?

Einstein was asked, "What was your greatest invention? Was it the theory of relativity?" His reported response was, "No. It was when I figured out compound interest." Even Einstein, who is still considered a great genius, didn't realize at one time during his life that the cost of money has a real value. Even if you just take $100 every month and put it somewhere toward your future, that $100 is going to be worth more in time thanks to compound interest.

An example of how compound interest works

In saving, there's a principle called "the rule of 72." Fundamentally, this rule lets you determine how long an investment will take to double given a fixed annual rate of interest. To demonstrate, we'll use the example of eating out in restaurants. Let's say that you have made the decision to eat out only twice a month instead of every week, which gives you the opportunity to save $100 every month. As you'll notice, you're not cutting out on something you enjoy (dining out). You're simply cutting down on the number of times that you do it. If you start at 25, what you'll accumulate by the time you've reached 55 is incredible.

$100 a month × 12 months = $1,200 a year + the interest.

$1,200 a year × 10 years = $12,000 + the interest.

By the time you reach 55 years old, that $100 a month has grown into $36,000 + the interest or possible dividends.

Continue doing that even longer, and perhaps you'll start to think about spending less time working and more time simply doing the things that you enjoy, and you'll have accumulated a large amount of savings without even having really thought about it. And more importantly, without even having missed the $100 a month.

One benefit of growing a network marketing business on a part-time basis is that you'll actually have the opportunity to make and save more money, while investing in yourself, as we'll learn from Foster.

Thoughts from Foster ...

My definition of building a better future always begins with investing in yourself. It's what's required to start things moving forward. That said, you also need a strong reason for planning for your future. Without a great and powerful reason, it's hard to get motivated. Investing in yourself means that you have to realize that there are things that you're going to have to learn, which brings me to my points:

1. Invest in yourself.
2. It's imperative to have enough reasons to look into the future.
3. Invest in people, because whether it's a company or an organization of some sort, it takes more than one voice to get things done. It's all about teamwork and collaboration.
4. Make a contribution.

Principle 11: Build a Better Future—Starting Today

Earlier this week, I had a conference call, and even though someone else was leading the call, from time to time I felt compelled to throw in some ideas. At the same time, I was listening to the ideas of the other people on the call. Just like the great company that we represent, there's not one factor in what we do that can be called a one-person show. There are people with great ideas from every walk of life and in all stages of their development. Collective ideas from other people help to build a better future. Sometimes you begin with what you think is a great idea, and by listening to others you soon realize that your idea has been transformed into a better idea simply by the act of listening to someone else's perspective.

Setting goals is something that I believe helps to build a better future, because then you have something to measure progress by. Otherwise it's just time wasted. Days, weeks, months, even years can go by without being able to measure whether or not progress is being made.

Whether the goals are small or big, they are important. Look at habits as an example. A simple habit is to not throw trash on the street. If everyone had the habit to throw trash where it belongs, in the garbage, this would go a long way toward helping us have a better, cleaner environment. The littering laws that we have today, in contrast to some countries, are a result of someone thinking about habits such as throwing garbage on the street years ago. Habits play a key role in building a better future. And of course, I'm referring to good habits here.

Making a contribution also plays a key role in the advancement of all things worthwhile. This is where we as individuals come in, because everyone's contribution is important—from the single person who makes sure to put their garbage in the trash can to the garbage collectors who make sure there are no piles of trash on our streets.

Again, we can mention the people like Henry Ford, Steve Jobs, and Bill Gates. These are all great minds. But the assembly-line worker who may not have a great invention to display contributes equally to the finished product by the daily work actions necessary to complete the project.

CHAPTER 12

Principle 12: Lead with Integrity

Integrity is a powerful word. It defines not only how an individual chooses to live their life but also who they are as a person. Integrity speaks about doing the right thing and taking the right action, no matter who is watching—and especially when *no one* is watching. More than that, though, integrity conjures up feelings of goodness, the "warm fuzzies." A capacity to trust yourself.

True leaders—whether it be a businessperson, politician, or parent—lead with integrity. Not only do they set the example for others, but their sense of integrity sets the direction and standard for their own lives. In many ways, integrity can be a guiding light, no matter what the circumstances or situation. On a fundamental level, your sense of integrity will always guide your actions. A simple example to demonstrate this is when a clerk hands you back your change and you realize that they've miscalculated and given you more than they should have. Do you bring this to their attention, or do you say nothing and walk out of the store? In the moment you may consider both before making a decision. *"Should I keep the money? Should I say something?"*

Should is an interesting word. It props you on the fence for a few seconds as you consider which side to lean toward. Those few moments of *should* are filled with the little voice inside our brains. It sways between excuses and justifications ("It's not HER money. This item is overpriced anyway") and a sense of responsibility

("Her cash register won't balance at the end of the day. What if she has to make it up from her own pocket?")

We all know what the "right thing to do is" regardless of whether the consequences are big or small. When you lead with integrity, you live knowing that you'll always do the right thing. This provides a calmness that settles deep within our core. The voice in our brain mentioned earlier lives with a constant fear of judgment. Living with integrity also provides a sense of confidence, because when you know you're doing the right thing by others and yourself, what other people think is not your concern.

Thoughts from John ...

One of the first people in this industry to make an impression on me was Mark Hughes, the founder of Herbalife International. As someone who genuinely cared about people, Mark had a philosophy. Whenever you met with him about anything to do with your business, he always wanted you to walk away feeling good about yourself, feeling good about him, and feeling good about the company. This to me is a great example of someone leading with integrity. Simply put, he cared.

Similar to that, my upline during my Herbalife days and someone who is a very good friend of mine to this day had a financial issue where a consultant believed that he was owed money. As it turned out, the consultant had made an honest mistake, and yet the company went ahead and paid him anyway when he questioned why he didn't get paid on something—even though it was his mistake.

Both of these examples demonstrate situations where it was more important to care about people than it was to care about making a profit. And this goes a long way. I strongly believe that

Principle 12: Lead with Integrity

when you care about the people, the profit will eventually follow. This is the philosophy that I've followed throughout the course of my entire career. It's very rare that I will turn down an opportunity to help someone by sharing my knowledge and experience in this industry. Even if it's someone from another company where I don't earn an income. Whether it's to answer questions or be involved on a conference call to offer advice on whatever challenges someone may be facing, I've always felt that it's important to help people above everything else. And when you do that, the benefit, whether it's monetary or the opportunity to learn something new, will find you. I consider it a type of karma.

In the 1990s, there was an article written about me in *Lifestyles* Magazine, and the interviewer came up with a caption that I never forgot: "Solleder loves people more than he loves money." During our talk and by me answering his questions, the writer had ascertained that this was the reason why I was so successful. And he was right. I think that's what it really comes down to. I genuinely love to see people succeed. I love to see people do something of value with their life. This is how I define leading with integrity: sincerely caring for others and wanting to help them.

I've coached people that have made more money in the industry than I have. And they'll tell you that I coached them and helped them and that I still help them to this day. I think that's what's really important. When you lead with integrity, everything falls into place. Taking that one step further, this is also the kind of people you attract so that you end up building a team of like-minded people with shared values.

A good tester for that is the question, "If this business did not exist, would I still want to know you?" Answering *yes* to that question says as much about you as it does about the people you surround yourself with. I feel fortunate that the people in my business are genuine; they don't just have dollar signs in their eyes. I've intentionally built my business on a solid foundation by leading with integrity. As a result, my team cares about other people. They care about the products. And they care about the company that they represent. All of this combined is as important for the brand as it is for our respective businesses.

When you give me your hard-earned money to buy my product, it matters to me that you get results. If you're going to trust me and join my team, again, tangible results are important. To me, that's selling from a place of integrity. This is how I've built my business. It's how I encourage my consultants to grow their business. And as they say, the proof is in the pudding. I refuse to exploit people's desire for health or success or whatever it is that one of my products or business opportunities promises. When you do something that you believe in, everything falls into place. Caring for others and helping them achieve their goals. That's what this business is all about.

Thoughts from Foster ...

Integrity goes beyond moral ethics because it affects every aspect of our lives. Recently, I was giving some thought to some of the things that we already know are associated with integrity: honesty, being trustworthy. I believe that integrity goes deeper than that. It also involves character and a willingness to work on the areas that a person may need growth in or further awareness. This is where integrity allows a person to continually evolve as a human being. I believe that this is where a real sense of integrity begins. If you think that you're "perfect" or that you know everything, then you

Principle 12: Lead with Integrity

aren't working from a place of value or a place of really trying to make things work for everyone involved. Integrity is the foundation of all relationships.

From a business point of view, I look at the decisions that I make on a daily basis and how they impact the people in my life. It has always been very important that I am sensitive in certain areas. In particular, I work at reserving judgment. I know that as a person I have my own individual faults, and with integrity, I truly work on those areas where I have to be very, very sensitive to avoid judging others. Learning and being aware is an area where integrity comes with humility, because we can all learn from other people. A child can even be a teacher as you observe their innocence and the way that they openly ask questions. True leaders understand and accept that they don't have all the answers.

Courage also plays a role in a person's integrity, as we learn to not be ashamed to say, "I don't know." There's nothing wrong in not knowing and accepting this reality that gives you an opportunity to learn and discover.

Another aspect of integrity is forgiveness. This is one area that I think a lot of people don't truly understand. Forgiveness plays a huge role in a person's ability to succeed, whatever success means to them personally. People will sometimes say the wrong thing and unintentionally offend someone because their words were not chosen well or were perceived in a certain way.

For example, this week I was put in a situation where I had to answer questions for a person that is evaluating our company. During our conversation this person said, "I've never even heard of you." The way that they said it—or the way that I understood what they were saying—was that because they had never heard of me, they were undermining both our company and my accomplishments. At some point I felt that I needed to boost my own ego, and I suggested that I introduce him to someone in our company that knows me very well. I knew that this person would speak highly of me.

What actually ended up happening was that the person evaluating our company found out that I had achieved Executive Diamond status much faster than other individuals that joined the business years before I did. Because of my need to boost my own ego at that time, what ended up happening is that I indirectly and unintentionally put someone else down. Of course, that's not what I meant to do, but it was a good lesson for me. An opportunity to learn something about myself and grow from that. In this case I needed to forgive myself. As well, I needed to seek forgiveness from the person whose efforts I had unintentionally undermined.

To give you the context of this situation, the person that was evaluating our company was asking specific questions to help him decide whether he should join my team or a different team. Understandably, he needed to know if I had what it takes to sponsor him. His specific question triggered something in me—my ego—making me feel that I needed to brag, and that wasn't what I wanted to do. Meanwhile, I was saying to myself, "Oh my goodness. I hope that this doesn't sound like I'm putting someone else down."

If this was done the other way around, I would have to be in a position to forgive. So, forgiveness is very, very important. This to me is part of integrity. Knowing your worth is important, but to a greater degree you have to also know your boundaries. When you lead with integrity, you know when to stop and you don't cross the line. Humility is key. People with integrity understand humility. I always say that it's far more impactful when people learn about your qualities or accomplishments without you having to tell them. When you don't have humility, you become an impostor to yourself and a servant to nobody. I would rather be a great servant who is playing a leadership role and have someone find out that, wow, this person can actually reach down to give someone a helping hand.

The ability to apologize also takes integrity. What often happens is that people tend to hold onto feelings of resentment, and this is unfair both to themselves and to the other person—all because someone refused or neglected to apologize.

As humans, we all have our shortcomings. No one is perfect. With integrity, the goal is to be whole. Even when you fail, the question should always be, "What do I do when I fail?" In other words, "When integrity fails, what do I do?" The answers are found in an ability to continue, to live with a sense of hope, and to forgive yourself and the other person. The words make it sound easy because they're simple, but it's not easy. We have to learn how to put aside our pride.

This is about checking what I call our blind spots with a willingness to work in the areas where we feel weak or vulnerable. We all have some variation of dysfunctions; they exist in all of us. Accepting responsibility for our mistakes and our weaknesses takes integrity.

Most importantly, people with integrity are kind. They care about others. Although considered a characteristic, this is actually an important tool, because when you genuinely care about other people, everything from humility to forgiveness comes easily.

CHAPTER 13

Principle 13: Success Doesn't Just Happen. Success Happens Just

Before we dig into this principle, we ask that you reread the title of this chapter and let the meaning of the words sink in.

This chapter is about doing the right things—taking the right actions—because truly, success is not a random outcome. You can't simply "wish" for success. It is the result of actions, mindset, and commitment. Even so-called overnight success stories are created from behind the scenes. Suddenly, a rock star seems to be everywhere. While waiting in line at the grocery store, you notice an actress is on the cover of every magazine. An author with a new best-selling book is being interviewed by all the top shows and podcasts.

The truth behind every one of these scenarios is that the musician, actress, and author all worked very hard and for a long time to get in the spotlight that is their current reality. They practiced their dream until it became a talent. When the shiny objects of their distractions tried to lull them onto an easier path, they reminded themselves of *why* their vision was so important to them. On the days when they felt overwhelmed and that they were just spinning their wheels, they went to bed tired and woke up the next morning, refreshed and ready to continue with even more determination.

Thoughts from John ...

I say this often and am never afraid of sounding like a broken record because it is so important: The first rule of our business is to always care more about your team of consultants than you do about yourself.

Make sure that your people make money, and if you have a mutual contact that's interested in joining your company, make sure that that person goes underneath the person underneath you. Greed has no place in this business, and you always want to be doing the right thing.

Reality check. Sometimes you have to go out of your way to do the right thing. Sometimes you have to make sacrifices to do the right thing. Sometimes it will cost you money to do the right thing. And when doing the right thing is from the heart, none of that will matter. The consequences will fall in your favor. When you do the right thing, not only does it buy you goodwill, but it also buys you credibility. It shows your integrity, and the way that you treat people goes a long way in revealing what kind of person you are.

Treating people with respect and being giving of my time has always been important to me. And purely from the nature of this business model, when you care about your team and make sure that your people are making money, you'll make money. This is the only industry I know of that rewards people for being truly unselfish. When your priorities are focused on others, everything always falls into place for you as well. It all goes back to the Golden Rule that we all learned as children: *Do unto others as you would want done unto you.*

There are a lot of universal rules that apply when you're in the people business. Do the right thing, and it will always come back to you. It may not come back to you today; it may only come back to you five or ten years down the road, but it will come back to you. As they say, serve others and you will eventually serve yourself.

Success doesn't just happen, success happens just. What that means is we're always praying for success, but things don't always turn out the way that we want them to. Once again, success will eventually follow you when you do the right things. The word "just" in this context stands for "justice." Justice is always served by doing the right thing for other people, for your customers, for your consultants, and for your company. When you do the right thing, it will always come back to serve you in a just manner.

A great example of doing the right thing for your people is being giving of your time. When you're dealing with people in a specific market, perhaps in a different time zone, sometimes you have to schedule a conference call at a time that's not convenient for you. By making yourself available to care for the people who need you "right now," you're serving them. You're also serving whoever they want you to meet. By making yourself available, it eventually comes back to you in a just way.

Another example is that sometimes it costs us money. Do I really want to make this trip to meet with a new consultant when I don't know how serious this person is? The key to our business is that behind every door, we never know who we're going to meet. Sometimes it's by accident. You may be traveling for a meeting and stop to put gas in your car, or you might sit next to someone on an airplane and it ends up that that person is a great prospect. Perhaps they're looking for a way to earn extra income. Perhaps they're interested in your products. And here you would have never met them if you weren't taking this trip. This is how things equal out in a just way.

A third example is, in my case I'm always checking volume at the end of the month to make sure that people are qualifying for their rank. I've done this ever since I started in this business years ago to make sure that no one leaves money on the table that they could earn and may not be aware of. Years ago, I was in senior management for a company, and I created a bimonthly pay system where I got on the phone and let individuals know how much sales volume they needed to make the next level and percentage of money. (This was before computers.)

People want to make money. That's why they're in business. And sometimes you, as the more experienced person, need to take care of that for them by pointing it out simply because they aren't aware. As someone who leads with integrity, this is actually your responsibility. And again, the benefits flow back to you. All because you took the time to care about someone else.

Thoughts from Foster ...

Success doesn't just happen, so it is important to understand that achieving success takes time. If it were easy, everyone would be successful. But because it takes time, you need to be aware of where you focus your energy. This is because whatever you focus on is where your energy goes. So, you want to make sure that you work on the things that really help you to stay consistent and create momentum.

I honestly believe that doing certain things and staying focused makes all the difference. The first one is that you must have faith. Life will throw you off course sometimes, and it will take faith to keep you on track and focused on your goals.

Along the same lines, you must have courage—the courage to believe in yourself. When we say, "believe in yourself," we don't mean you cannot believe in anyone else. We're talking about fighting the "enemy within," which is YOU. If you doubt yourself, it doesn't matter how much courage you have or what encouragement people give you, because you will eventually give up. It is therefore imperative that you believe in yourself and in the reasons why you are striving to attain whatever goal you've set your mind on.

You want to get into a habit of never giving up on yourself, no matter what. I believe that the true definition of failure is when you give up on yourself. It's one thing to be fired from a job, but if you are running your own show (which is part of what this book is about, taking control of your life), you need to develop into the type of person that takes charge.

Taking charge of your life also means that you have to be mindful of the people you surround yourself with. You cannot surround yourself with negative people. You also have to accept the fact that you simply can't please everybody. At the end of the day, you are your own strength.

We all have that strength within us, but when you start focusing on all the negative energy coming at you, it is going to strip you of your own strength and weaken you. We all have this fight in us. It's a positive fight. It's a fight where you don't want to go down easy. You should never just throw in the towel. You have to give it your all, and I call this "the battle until the end." You have to really do everything you can that is within your power to make it happen.

We all have days where it's difficult to put on a smile, but some days that's what you must put on in order to win the fight. You don't want to suppress anything, but at the same time, if you focus on the negative, you will attract the wrong people.

Part of staying focused to get that energy going is making sure that you're doing the right thing. This includes having integrity. Integrity is not for anyone else. It is for you, because again, if you're not true to yourself, you'll find it very, very difficult and you'll feel as though life is turning on you. And when life gives you some of those daily challenges, it will take integrity to do the right thing.

We all have many reasons why we do what we do. This is where you need your personal WHY to help you to do the right thing. It's not about your responsibilities as a family man, for example, or as an individual contributing to society. For sure we're all here to contribute, to make a difference. And it takes all these reasons to do the right thing. If we lived in a society where we weren't law-abiding and we could just ignore everything, then of course life would be chaotic.

If we don't achieve what we need to one day, there is always tomorrow. I believe that if you're doing the right thing, you don't need to rush and think that everything must be finished today. If you're looking into the future and you're working on something that's going to have long-lasting rewards, you have to look at every day as, "Okay. I didn't get it all done today, but I will do better next time." Having the attitude that there's always tomorrow is a very good thing.

You definitely must love what you do, particularly in business, because if you do what you love, then success will follow. It is very difficult to go through your days doing something that you don't enjoy. I know that sometimes, temporarily, we have to do what we must in order to survive and pay the bills. But I'm saying that if you're going to do something for yourself, particularly in business, make sure that you love what you do; otherwise you are going to eventually give up. Running a business is a full-time commitment. Even if you're doing it part-time, it's still a full-time commitment. And that decision has to be made from the get-go. This is all part of doing the right thing.

This brings me to my final point, which I call "the timeline." This is about having the right attitude. Every day that we face is a

Principle 13: Success Doesn't Just Happen. Success Happens Just

day that we'll never get back. Whether you're 30 years old or 60, every single day must count. It must mean something. This is where I agree with Tony Robbins when he says that you must have this "must attitude" all the time. This doesn't mean that you won't have setbacks, but you must continue to press forward regardless of those inevitable setbacks.

Sometimes I like to go back and remind myself of the got-to attitude. There was a time when my wife and I were living in a two-bedroom apartment. For us, buying a home became a priority. We had made a written statement about buying a home, but we didn't have any money; we had nothing saved and I didn't know how we were going to buy a home. But one day I said to my wife, "We're going to buy a house." And she asked, "How?"

I made the decision to meet with a mortgage specialist and I showed him what I was doing at the time and how much money I was earning. I was in my second year in business, and he looked at the regular checks coming in, and even though my credit wasn't the greatest, he was able to arrange a mortgage and he assured me that within three months we would be moving into a home. And because buying a home had become a "must" for me, it happened. Within three months, my wife and I had bought our first home.

CHAPTER 14

Principle 14: Imagine that this is Your Last Chance

While the title of this chapter may seem negative or pessimistic, it's actually not. Like a deadline or a due date, it's meant to serve as the kick in the butt that many of us need. Not to insinuate that we're lazy or irresponsible. It's simply human nature to put things off until we've reached the proverbial "end." Or in this context, the last chance to plan for the future that we want or to accomplish a long-desired goal.

Thoughts from John ...

The truth is that it's never an actual last chance. As they say, you only fail when you don't get back up and try again. However, when it comes to finances and saving for your retirement or your children's education, if you haven't started, you're already late in the game, no matter what your age is. I say this because I'm of the firm belief that you should start saving for your future as soon as you start earning an income. I call this "paying yourself first." While this is a discipline, it's unfortunately something that most of us aren't taught.

If you have not saved for your future, the first thing you need to deal with is the reality of your circumstances. How old are you? At what stage are you in your life? For example, if you're 50 years old and you haven't saved a dime, it's not too late. It simply means that you need to economize or compress time. Someone who is 33 years old has about 30 years to save for their future. Someone who is 50 realistically has about ten years. This doesn't necessarily mean that you stop earning income in your later years. It just means that you should focus on building income that hopefully is residual within that ten-year timeframe.

The first step is to ask yourself how much you'll need in the future to figure out how much you need to start saving today. If you're 50 years old and you figure that you will be retiring at age 70, which is a realistic number in this day and age, that gives you 20 years to put money away. After taxes and expenses, saving $50,000 a year is a good number to invest in your retirement years. That may seem like a lot of money, and it is. It's approximately $4,000 a month. That's what you need to put away per month so that at the end of the year you have $50,000 that's going to sit there and accumulate interest. This is an example of number crunching.

The next step is to plan. Where will this "extra" money come from? Assuming you currently have a job that covers your expenses (mortgage, car payment, various insurance payments, putting food on the table, vacations, etc.), you realize that there's not a lot of money left at the end of the month. Without compromising on quality of life, you realize that you need to start a home-based business. Are you going to quit your job? The answer to that is a definite NO, for many reasons. Perhaps your job provides you with benefits. The second reason is that quitting your job would take you away from the people that you already know and from the opportunity to meet other people. You're starting a home-based and solitary business to create a multiple source of income, not to replace your current salary.

Principle 14: Imagine that this is Your Last Chance

A lot of times your co-workers become your friends. You socialize with them. Go have a drink with them after work, or you're in a bowling league together. Using the network marketing business model as an example, it is a people business. You can mention your offering and you don't even have to recruit them, but they may become customers, especially when you have a genuine belief in the company and products that you represent. Quitting your job would be what's called "premature full-time." Unfortunately, a lot of people do this. They quit their job and focus full-time on their home-based business. What ends up happening is that they get stressed. It takes time to build a business, and how can you focus on your business when you're worried about paying your bills? A better question is, how can you focus on saving for the future when you're struggling to pay your current living expenses?

As well, it takes time to develop the skills required for growing a business. That said, the right action to take is to keep your job so that you keep a regular income coming in. Your "side hustle" is addition, not equalization or subtraction. You want to ADD to the kitty, not replace it. Not yet. And this is how you compress time: by knowing your numbers.

One of the things I've observed about the superstars in business—the people who have built big businesses, whether it's in direct selling or it's in owning another type of business model—is that they know their numbers:

- They know what they need to sell.
- They know what they need to sell to pay the bills.
- They know what they need to sell as an extra to be able to save.

As entrepreneurs, we need to know our numbers, because otherwise we don't know what we're working for. Using the example mentioned earlier, knowing that we need to save $50,000 a year helps to keep us going. It gives us a target, a number to strive for. Meanwhile, you have your regular day job to cover today's expenses. Unfortunately, most people don't think strategically. This is why so many people wind up 70 years old and without the money they need to cover basic expenses. Meanwhile, they've made a lot of money in their lives. And here's the sad part: If they added up all the money that they've made during their lifetime, they'd realize that they've made a hell of a lot of money and have no idea where it all went.

You paid taxes. You paid your expenses. You paid your rent or your mortgage and your car payment and your insurance, and so on. But you never learned to pay yourself first. The reason people fail is that they don't have a target; they don't know where they're going; they don't know what it is that they're working for. Then the minute it gets a little hard or difficult, they quit because they forget the reason they started in the first place. Realistically, whether you're selling vitamins or homes, most people don't start off because that's what they want to do. They do it because they want to get somewhere in life. Your reason reminds you that you want to get somewhere else in your life. You do it for your future.

Thoughts from Foster ...

This is a big subject that I think anybody, myself included, can appreciate. If you're looking at something as though it's your "last chance," you definitely want to be the very best at every single thing that you do. One thing that I know I would do is put more time into the things that matter to me the most. I feel very fortunate to have found my true passion in life. Helping average people to become superheroes is something that gives me the greatest joy. And being

Principle 14: Imagine that this is Your Last Chance

in this industry, referred to as network marketing or multi-level marketing, makes it possible for me to do that. I realize that there are many opportunities out there, yet this particular industry makes it possible for me to help the average person to become a superhero of their own life.

One of the things I would do if it was my last chance is that I would sacrifice more. I think that sometimes we're a little too selfish. This morning I did something that I think is worth sharing here. What's interesting is that just two weeks ago my wife and I were chatting, and I asked her, "How would you define love?" Without digressing here, today I demonstrated real sacrificial love. Here's what happened.

A friend of mine who also happens to be in the network marketing business had been living in Jamaica for quite some time and came back for a visit. A week later she needed to get to the airport in time to catch her flight at 9 a.m. And when I was discussing with my wife that I would be giving her a ride, it meant I would have to leave our house at 5 a.m. to get to her place at 5:30 a.m. to be able to get her to the airport at 6 a.m.

I was describing that love to my wife and I said, "This is not the romantic kind of love, but it's one of those types of love that you render to a friend or to a neighbor. It's like, love your neighbor as yourself; something that you do for yourself that you wish somebody else would do for you when needed."

All that to say that if I was considering this my "last chance," I would sacrifice more of my time for others. I truly mean that. Instead of focusing on myself, I would be of service to humanity. I would also spend more time—in quantity and quality—with loved ones. I think it's important to understand that considering any time in your life as your "last chance" is an opportunity to make changes right now.

With my "last chance" as the focal point, I would put more focus on what's important to me, including my faith, my family, my work, and all the things that I believe we spend a lot of time pursuing. My biggest change is that I would be more intentional. What I mean by that is, if it's my health, I would make that intentional living. If it's about my work, I would be more intentional about what I do. In other words, I would attend more network marketing events. I would make it very intentional; put in the effort to seek out more knowledge. And also taking more risks. Because sometimes we like to play it safe, and that's not necessarily a good thing. How can we learn and grow if we're always playing it safe?

Also, as my last chance I would make sure to practice being grateful more often. I appreciate my wife in so many ways, and because of this, she is very appreciative of what I call the love nest. Whatever act of kindness she receives, she will call, even if I'm in a meeting, and say, "Thank you. I really appreciate that." Sometimes that act of kindness is returned, even though you don't expect anything back: They call you to say "Thank you for being there. Thank you for helping. Thank you for listening. Thank you for giving me that shoulder to lean on."

When we know that this is our last opportunity, we shouldn't even be afraid to correct things. For example, I have what I refer to as "forgive and be free." There are so many of us that are hurt by many different people. And sometimes we carry that burden. To have the courage to say to somebody, "I'm wrong. I'm sorry," or "Please forgive me." If this is my last opportunity and my last chance, I would like to resolve things and to make peace.

Another intention for my "last chance" would be to do the things that help to build people up. To be more intentional in the way that I praise my own kids is a good example. Sometimes they're doing great things, and they don't always receive the praise that they deserve. To be able to say, "I'm proud of you" or "I know you can do it." These are simple things that will make somebody's day.

Thinking that this may be your last chance makes you truly look at yourself and your life and realize that you can start doing all of these things even if it's not really your last chance. This can make you a better person. Sometimes we need to press pause. Sometimes we need to just halt and ask ourselves, "Why am I doing all this?" In other words, if something that you're doing is not making this planet a better place, better than you and I found it, we definitely need to press pause.

There are also aspects in our lives and in ourselves that we would not change. I'll continue to love my wife. I'll continue to love my kids. I'll continue to love my friends and neighbors. But what I would do differently are the things that I've listed. And this topic also makes me more aware to be more mindful. I don't have to wait until my very last day or last chance. My last day could be today; it could be this minute. So why not be intentional about every single minute?

CHAPTER 15

Principle 15: Get Ready for Your Next Level

Reaching the next level is a highly personal goal. For some, it means attaining financial freedom. For others, the next level has nothing to do with finances and everything to do with reaching a certain status, whether that's a degree, title, or position. Regardless of what reaching the next level means to you, it comes down to values and personal ambitions. Reaching the next level is about a sense of achievement and peace of mind.

Our hope with this book and the principles we've defined throughout is that they will help you to set standards for yourself with a roadmap to achieving the life you want.

Thoughts from John ...

Life has many variables and even an order to them. For me, it's faith first. Then health, family, and finances. That said, because my expertise is in finances, I'm going to start with that. In order to get your finances together, you need to take an interest in interest. Wealthy people earn interest. Poor people pay interest. The question is, which do you want to be: wealthy or poor? Obviously, the answer is wealthy, or at least financially secure. And the first step in getting there is paying off your financial debts. This includes credit cards, lines of credit, and overdraft accounts. Basically, anything that you pay interest on and that is not considered an investment. Once you've paid off your financial debts, you benefit from a freedom that most people never get to experience. Can you imagine what your life would be like if you had no debt?

The next step is to accumulate assets for your future. You invest today with tomorrow in mind. Of course, you may have to skip a few things (like the daily latte) and you have to be disciplined so that you don't end up at age 65 wondering how you're going to pay for your basic living expenses. No one wants to end up like that. Once again, you have to be disciplined every day, and sometimes discipline is painful. Not to demean what women go through during childbirth, but I like to use this as an example to convey both ends of the spectrum. During childbirth, the pain is excruciating. This is what discipline feels like. Once the child is born, it's the most wonderful feeling in the world. And that's what living debt-free feels like.

Sometimes the pain that we have to go through … the pain of discipline … the pain of not being able to do some of the things that other people are doing … everyone is going on vacation … everyone is going to expensive restaurants. This is where discipline comes in: where you may need to put some money into a retirement account or your children's education fund or an old-age fund. Instead of living in the moment, we need to plan for the future.

And then there's the hard yet realistic question: What if I'm planning for the future and I suddenly die tomorrow? I will have missed out on some of the things I love today. But let's flip that around. If you don't die tomorrow (and odds are that you won't), then what's going to happen down the road in terms of your life when you want that money to be there to take care of yourself in your later years or to take care of your kids? This is where we

Principle 15: Get Ready for Your Next Level

need to start thinking a little differently than we have in the past. It's about having the discipline to invest, to save and put money away. It's sometimes even the discipline to continue with our day job although we're not enjoying it.

Now that I'm older, I often get asked when I plan to stop working. And that includes the daily calls, traveling, and promoting my business and its offering in terms of opportunity and products. My answer is never, because I don't know when that rainy day is going to come. It may never come, but I want to be prepared, and the best way to be prepared is by keeping my sword sharpened. As an aside, I feel fortunate that what is considered my "work" is something that I believe in and feel passionate about.

This is where a lot of people make a mistake. They get a certain amount of income or a certain amount of money and they think they can then take it easy. They start coasting. The problem with coasting is that your skills get rusty very fast. It's consistent with going to the gym. If you've never gone to the gym and you go for the first time, it's a joyous experience. It's like, "Wow! Look at this equipment. Look at this treadmill. This is all fun." But if you're like me and you've been a gym rat your entire life, you know how painful it is when you stop for whatever reason and start up again. The easier way is to continue. To follow a schedule and stick with it.

It's the same thing in business. If you continue to grow and continue to work it by putting in the time and effort, you're never going to have that difficulty of "How the heck do I get started again?" As humans we're lazy. We look for the path of least resistance. The good news is that the easy way is to keep doing it. That said, if you want to cut back on the hours or trips that you take, that's another story. But you don't ever want to stop developing your skills and growing as a person—both from a business perspective and as a human being. It's important to remember that you're a student your entire life. The day that you stop learning is the day that you stop living.

In relation to the next level, your ambitions and even your knowledge and skills, it's all part of a journey. The journey is the bigger picture. And that's what most people don't understand. They see the accumulation of achievements and self-development as an amount, like when a glass is full. They think, "when I can retire" or "when I can go to the beach" or "when I can go fishing whenever I feel like it." These are all nice things to do, but the reality of it is that we never forget the skills that got us to where we are today. And if you keep developing those skills and never stop sharpening that proverbial sword, your next level also continues to expand. You don't want your skills to diminish as you get older. If anything, they should get better.

Years ago, for a short period of time I sold life insurance. It's one of the few things I've done throughout my career that was outside of multi-level. Although I only did this for a short time, I'll never forget the impact it had on me. I worked with a man who was 70 years old and was considered a living legend with the Metropolitan Life Insurance Company. I used to get to the office very early in the morning, around 5:30 or 6. One morning I arrived to find him already there. He had come back from writing an application on a client. I remember asking why he still worked. His response was, "As I've gotten older, my business has gotten easier because I've gotten better at it."

It's only today that I truly have an understanding of what he was trying to say to me. I've been working in the network marketing industry for over 37 years. Do you think I'm better at it now than I was 35 years ago? I had better be. Financially, I don't have as much of a need as I've had at other times in my life, and yet I continue to work at it every day. Just today, I've already done eleven conference calls, and I still have three more tonight. Not only that, but I went to the gym and still made sure to spend time with my kids. My point is that you can do it all in life, but only if you focus on getting the job done each and every day.

That's how you get to the next level. The good news is that the next level is always easier than the last level because you're bringing everything you've learned and worked for with you. There was a study done which came to the conclusion that if you take a person who has made a million dollars and you take away all their money, within twelve months they'll make it again. Why? Because the skill they developed to make it in the first place is still there.

On the other hand, a person that has never made a million dollars doesn't know how to make it; they're still guessing at it. It's the skill development that's going to make it a second, third, or fourth time in a career. Throughout every next level, your foundation is stronger than the level before. That alone is reason to never stop growing.

Thoughts from Foster ...

Regardless of what type of business you're in, whether you're in real estate or network marketing, every entrepreneur must have what I call a routine, and to get to that level, you must nail down certain points that I believe will bring growth. Following are the top four that I focus on and that have helped me grow my business.

1. Daily number of contacts

It goes without saying, yet it's still an important reminder, that to get any business or endeavor to the next level, you cannot just sit down and cross your fingers and expect things to happen. You need to have daily habits. And to do that, you need to get into action mode where you treat your business like it's a start-up every single day. This applies to everything, from learning an instrument to preparing for a marathon. At some point and on some days, the excitement won't be there, yet you still need to push through your daily routine.

This is because what we're talking about here is getting ready for the next step. And your next step cannot come to life without you doing certain things. So, there has to be this mindset of you treating your business as a start-up business. You have to give a business a good 24 months. The numbers don't really matter, because it all depends on what you have planned. The goal is to get your business going into what I call growth mode, and you can't do that unless you have this mindset of your business being a start-up.

This is where most people start, with all this enthusiasm and excitement and energy. With a start-up business you go in all excited, and you have to get in that mode every single day.

2. Daily number of appointments

If your contacts are just a bunch of business cards sitting on your desk, they won't do anything for you unless you send a message or pick up the phone and make an appointment. And of course, if you make enough appointments, you'll definitely create opportunities to do something that takes you to step #3.

3. Daily number of presentations

People need to hear and understand what you do and what you're offering, and the way to do that is to present it. A presentation doesn't always mean a formal PowerPoint, but you need to be able to present your ideas in a quantifiable way.

4. Daily number of follow-ups

I always refer to the fact that the fortune is in the follow-up. For example, today I did about six follow-up calls. Four of the people I reached out to were very happy that I called, because they wanted to know where we go from here. If I had just left it and expected them to call me, nothing would have moved forward.

So again, the number of follow-ups is really where the fortune is, because at the end of the day, every entrepreneur wants to get to the level that I call the cash cow. But you can't get to that cash cow until all the actions have taken place.

Your net worth equals your network, so if you have a small network, you're going to have a small net worth. You have to get yourself into the growth mode, and this means that you are all in, no matter what the weather is, no matter what is going on around you. Frankly, you're just doing everything you can; because if not, you'll just be fading away, and that to me is dangerous.

One of the things that is sometimes required is flexibility. For example, if technology is changing, you have to restructure some of your processes. You also have to be able to dominate. What I mean by that is that your community should know you and even count on you as the expert or the go-to person. For example, you can be in real estate and yet not know what's going on in your community. This is a mistake. Fixing it can be as simple as attending community events so that you position yourself within your market.

By following the four dailies (mentioned above) and guarding that routine against all distractions, I can guarantee that anyone can bring their business to the next level.

CHAPTER 16

And Now It's Up to You!

As we mentioned at the beginning of this book, our businesses and our relationships are built on our capacity to be straightforward, vulnerable, and supportive. It's what we expect from ourselves and it's what we *give* of ourselves. Sharing our experiences and insights with you has been a pleasure. Our goal with this book is to provide you with a solid foundation for taking your business and your life to the next level.

There's not a single person in this world that doesn't dream of a better life. It's human nature to aspire ... to endeavor ... to want control over our time, our finances, and our lives. We're living proof that building a network marketing industry provides the opportunity to have it all.

To give you an idea of the prominence of network marketing companies, including the long-standing organizations that have become household names over the years, a 2018 industry overview conducted by the Direct Selling Association (DSA) reported that Direct Selling in the United States alone represents $35.4 billion in retail sales. This number represents a 1.3% increase over 2017.

If you're wondering how, this answer can also be found in a DSA report, one that concluded that "77% of Americans are interested in flexible, entrepreneurial/income-earning opportunities." This position, building a direct marketing business as a top option since, as stated earlier, MLM is driven by two words: "Opportunity" and "Relationships."

It is our hope that you'll apply the principles outlined in this book to your daily life. From living with integrity to creating balance and waking up feeling excited for the day ahead. These are the true signs of success. And with the stats from DSA, it's clear that the opportunities are right in front of you.

And if you can't take our word for it, we reached out to other network marketers from various companies, backgrounds, and levels of experience. We asked them four questions:

What originally put you in a situation where you wanted to build your own business via MLM?
What obstacle(s) have you overcome since starting your MLM journey?
What is the best piece of advice you've received since joining?
Why do you believe everyone should consider MLM as a multiple source of income?

Their answers in the following pages reveal their personal experiences in this industry. It is with great pride that we say this industry is inclusive of all people. It doesn't matter what your past experience has been, where you live, or how old you are. Success is a brass ring that belongs to everyone, regardless of gender or race.

To your success and happiness,
John Solleder and Foster Owusu

CHAPTER 17

Meet the Many Faces of Our Industry

Every day, every hour, every minute, someone is introduced to the opportunity that is network marketing. Students looking for a way to make extra money as they continue with their studies. Single parents looking for a way to balance their time as they raise their children. Individuals looking for a way to nurture their entrepreneurial spirits. Network marketing provides an opportunity that is based on a foundation of building people while working on your own self-development. People helping people. That's the key to building a successful network marketing business.

In this section, we're happy to introduce you to inspiring people who, like you, were looking for a way to improve their lives. Some may say that they found the solution in network marketing. But truly, they found the solution inside themselves. Network marketing is simply a means, a vehicle. And like all vehicles, there's no movement without action. Success in this industry is driven by unique stories and motivations. These are people that have devoted their lives to an industry that offers limitless opportunities. More importantly, these are people that have devoted their lives to helping others improve their lives.

These are their stories.

Gabriella Ankrah, CANADA

What originally put you in a situation where you wanted to build an MLM (Multi-Level Marketing) business?

My excitement and arrival to Canada was short-lived when I quickly realised that as a foreign professional, I could not find a suitable job without any Canadian experience. My next option was to set up my own business, but I ran into a real-life difficulty, which was getting the heavy capital to start any conventional business.

Luckily, I called my uncle in Ottawa to get a loan and he connected me to a lady who had tried to get him into an MLM company. That started my journey with a network marketing business with my previous company. My husband and I got involved in it and worked hard and reached a level that I didn't have to search for a job or start a conventional business with a heavy capital investment that I did not have.

Secondly, starting the MLM business helped me to stay home and care for my kids while making money from home.

What obstacles have you overcome since starting your MLM journey?

In my previous company, we were advised not to call any situation an obstacle or problem but to address them as challenges.

Obstacles or problems sound more severe to tackle and are more into the negative side of affairs. So, in building a network business we face challenges just like anything we do in life. We deal with the most important "obstacle" every day, which is human beings.

If you take care of the number-one human being, yourself, and learn to be tolerant with others, whatever they do, you can overcome that challenge. The first books my senior associate recommended that I read were *Personality Plus* by Florence Littauer and *The Seven Habits of Highly Effective People* by Stephen R. Covey. These books really helped me to overcome the human challenges. With these two books and others I've read along the way, I've come to realise that extroverts and introverts can both build a business if they get into the self-development program by reading the recommended books.

"Self-development" is an important part of the networking business to help one overcome challenges—"obstacles." It is an integral part of the training of associates to help them to overcome the challenges we face in the building of an MLM business.

What is the best piece of advice you have received since joining?

Among other life knowledge that I have acquired through network marketing, one of the best pieces of advice given to me was to "NEVER LET ANYONE STEAL YOUR DREAM." This advice prepared me to be aware that people are very unkind in this world. When they cannot do something, they try hard to discourage you from succeeding in whatever you are doing, so I always advise my team members to be aware of the "DREAM STEALERS."

Focus on your dreams. If you don't have any, find one that will be your propeller to get you to succeed despite all challenges.

Why do you believe everyone should consider MLM as a multiple source of income?

1. MLM is on the top of the list of businesses and jobs that have created more millionaires and made a lot of families financially sustainable. All other businesses create one or at most two millionaires and a billionaire, so the wealth created is very individualistic. It is a one-family show, but in MLM, the wealth is shared with all who have dreams and are willing to achieve them through this method of creation.
2. With this bad economic situation that the pandemic is creating throughout the world, I believe the best thing for most people to do is to consider getting involved in an MLM business that is succeeding.
3. It costs the price of a good shoe or a suit to get involved in most MLM businesses, so it's very affordable.
4. In the job world or other conventional businesses, it's a dog-eat-dog affair, dirty competition; whereas in an MLM you are in for yourself but not by yourself. In a very successful MLM, the person that brings you in can only succeed when they help you to succeed. It's a win-win situation.
5. The world can be such a lonely place, but MLM can plug you into a worldwide family, apart from the money you will make.
6. If you ever want to get involved in a group of positive and trusting people, get involved in MLM, where you will find more people from that category than any other organization.
7. Most people don't have enough time, especially women, to be with their children as they grow up and teach them the values and ethics they want to impart to the children. An MLM business gives you the opportunity to work and take

care of your children, and you don't have to lie to get time off to attend to a sick child. Most people don't get time to go on their dream vacations in their lifetime because of work.

8. In MLM, if you have a big dream and are willing to work, you can succeed more than the person who brought you into the business.

There are so many benefits to building an MLM business that if people are open-minded and they look into it, they will be interested.

Mauricio Cuevas Arouesty, MEXICO–
English and Spanish

What put you in a situation where you wanted to build your own business through network marketing?
The advantages of the industry, the possibility that with low investments you can create wealth for a lifetime. The personal development that the industry brings to be able to bring as many people as possible to the best result of their lives. The low costs, and how simple and practical it is.

What obstacles have you overcome since you started your network marketing career?
I believe that one of the biggest obstacles I have faced in the industry is developing and changing the mindset of my team.

For example, when new people join, they have a lot of energy, enthusiasm, and determination. Yet many times, they pause their growth. So, finding the right words and actions to empower them has been one of my biggest challenges.

What is the best advice you have received since you started?
Do it with the heart, with the genuine intention to help people, and most importantly, make it SIMPLE. The person who comes

to network marketing solely to make money comes for VERY LITTLE. When you have your heart and all your talents in leading your team to the best result, I consider this the best advice I have received.

Why do you think everyone should consider network marketing as an option to receive additional income?
Because it is the largest industry worldwide, with the largest number of new millionaires. The personal development it gives you (I am devouring these books!) is amazing. For me, it's a win-win because of the residual income, the team, FREEDOM, etc. I AM DEFINITELY WHERE I WANT TO BE!

Angel Cardona, PUERTO RICO

What originally put you in a situation where you wanted to build your own business via MLM?
Being able to create a business that operates in multiple countries that in turn allows me to develop teams and entrepreneurs in those markets. I have always believed that your income cannot come from a single market.

What obstacle(s) have you overcome since starting your MLM journey?
The challenges I have encountered have been being able to show the potential distributor that we have an opportunity that meets what an entrepreneur has always looked for in an opportunity. Unique product, good price, guaranteed results, clinical evidence, a potentially lucrative plan, and management that understands Latino culture.

What is the best piece of advice you've received since joining?
The best advice I received and the one I always share is: We have to work more on ourselves as people and our leadership if we want to achieve high positions within the company's plan.

Why do you believe everyone should consider MLM as a multiple source of income?

We must consider the network marketing business as a legitimate business that operates in multiple countries. You can have free advice from your sponsors, who have created a business opportunity, because with less than $500 you can develop a way to be generating absurd income per month, and they will tell you what you need to do to achieve the same. It is a complete win-win.

Sandy Chambers, CANADA

What originally put you in a situation where you wanted to build your own business via MLM?
When I graduated from university, I thought I was going to set this world on fire. My goal was to teach. I loved it and did well with it. In my third year, I became head of my department, but my husband wanted a career in food chemistry and applied for positions all across the country. Because education was not federal, I had to start at the bottom in our new city. Not being totally happy with my new circumstances, I opted to stay home and raise a family. When my three young children were starting to go to school, I was ready to go back to work. I had always dreamed of owning my own business, wanting to see what my potential could look like. As I was putting out feelers for a job, a neighbour invited me to a cosmetic skin care party. I loved the whole concept, and before I knew it, I was an independent distributor. Working from home and around my family's needs was a perfect fit. I was with this company for 13 years, winning cars and gifts, but this was direct sales and I was limited to where I lived. To do the business, I had to be with the potential customer or distributor to literally put the product on her face. It was by no means a global business.

One Friday afternoon, I got a call from a friend who talked about a new company that was multi-level marketing. I was impressed with being paid many levels deep, rather than the two levels I was paid on. Also, I didn't have to sample the product. My world suddenly became much larger. I could contact people anywhere in my country. By this time, I was a single parent with three children entering university, so the raise in pay was very appealing. As it turned out, my monthly checks went from 4 to 5 digits almost from the beginning.

What obstacle(s) have you overcome since starting your MLM journey?

When you are in your own business, like any job, there are ups and downs. It's the downs that make you strong! That's where you learn valuable lessons. In my first business, my children were 4, 6, and 7 years old. They wanted my time, and for the most part I worked around their schedule. Then I found myself heading toward management. I had three months to double my business, and the push was on. My obstacle was getting my family on board with my goal. I designed a huge thermometer and promised them a three-week family vacation in Hawaii if I met my goal. I figured out what that would cost and put that number at the top of the thermometer. Each week, the kids coloured in how much I made toward the trip. It wasn't long before they were pushing me out the door to make more money. We did end up going to Hawaii and I became a Sales Director.

Another obstacle I had was a physical one. I got a call from a friend about this amazing opportunity that was just starting in my country. I really captured the vision and was very excited—enough to purchase the biggest package there was, and I had no way to pay for it if this didn't work out. I had taken time off for the past three months to look for something new and was running very low on cash. One thing in my favour was I did have a credit card with nothing on it. Before I received the product, I burned my foot. Hot bubbling fat at 450 degrees fell on my foot. I was sent home from the hospital bandaged with a bottle of painkillers. The instructions were to stay home and keep my foot elevated. Here I had all this product coming with no way to pay for it unless I sold it, and I couldn't drive because the drugs blurred my vision. As it turns out, this obstacle was the best thing that ever happened to me because I learned how to sponsor, how to sell the product and to become really good at closing the deal, and all over the phone. I paid for local couriers to pick up and deliver the boxes of product. Within the month, my business went into momentum. Instead of driving all over the city to see people, I could take that precious time to make many more calls than I ever thought possible. I started to expand my business by phone to all over the country. I have learned that obstacles are there to make us learn. I always believe that after your darkest times, your light shines stronger and better than before. I became known as the Closer because of that time where I learned so much out of necessity.

What is the best piece of advice you've received since joining?

After being in the industry for four decades, I do have a lot of advice. I have spent thousands of dollars to learn that your attitude is everything. If you can think it, you can do it. Everything is possible. You need a positive mindset and attitude to be successful. If you come into this industry to "try it" or to "let's see" what you can do, you will not be successful. You need to focus on being successful and not allowing one negative thought to penetrate your thinking. What you focus on, you get more of. If you are focusing on trying, you'll still be trying. If you focus on putting in the time with no clear goal, you'll probably be in the same place a year from now. You need to have clear goals of what you want and to feel what your life would look like when you achieve these goals. Don't worry how you are going to do it. Just take the first few steps, and new ideas will open up for you.

When I started my first truly successful business, I had no idea I would have thousands of people in my group. I didn't even know thousands of people. But I followed the marketing plan. Any good marketing plan will show you what you need to do. In this case, I had to find six people who could find one. That's what I concentrated on, and then helped them get their six. By then, my business was becoming so big, and another idea came to me. I should begin hotel meetings and then get other cities involved. Now this is many years ago, but we found ways to bring larger numbers of people together.

Today it would be done on the computer. My point is when you start acting on your goals, making things happen, ideas and opportunities to grow faster start to come to you.

My other advice is to find yourself a mentor. Don't do this alone. For one thing, it's not fun, but the other thing is a mentor can help you achieve success faster than you can learn on your own. I don't understand why so many people from many different careers think they don't need any training for network marketing. When I first started, someone said to me, "Do you think you could learn if I taught you how?" Being an educator, I knew I could learn, but I knew I had to be educated. I attended every training there was. I read books on it and I worked with people who were in the positions I wanted to be in. When choosing a mentor, make sure they are making the income you aspire to make and that they have reached the rank where you want to be. I remember a friend calling me one day, saying she discovered her daughter was going to hire a life coach. In questioning her daughter, she found out this coach made $10,000 a year, was divorced and living in her parents' basement. Her daughter, on the other hand, made over $100,000 a year, had a great marriage, and lived in her own home. What could this coach teach her? It is very important who you select to mentor you.

Why do you believe everyone should consider MLM as a multiple source of income?

MLM is a great solution for many people, whether you have a full-time job or not. I have seen so many people over the years take on a second job to make ends meet. What they don't consider is that the wages from the second job are taxable and often elevate that person to a higher tax rate. Sometimes their entire earnings from the second job go to the government in taxes! When you become an independent distributor in network marketing, you get all the tax benefits of a business owner. You can even write off some of your home and car expenses as well as many other things. I often suggest that people start their business while they have a job so that they have a wage coming in while they build their business. It is a business and does take some time to build, but it is so worth it.

To start a business in network marketing, it usually has a low entrance fee and monthly costs, unlike most businesses, but also has a very large upside. There is no ceiling on what you can make. Everyone comes into the industry with a different skill set, but everyone can learn. Unlike many corporate jobs, the people you work with want you to succeed, get the same job as them, and are willing to train you for free. You learn while you earn. It's important to pick your mentor and the person you join the business with, because you will be spending a lot of time with them.

Thousands of people a day are starting a network marketing business all over the world to change their lives for the better or to establish some financial security. Over the years when the economy is unsettled and people are losing their jobs, network marketing thrives. Due to the advances in technology, jobs are changing; some are actually becoming extinct. Network marketing offers a plan B for those who feel their jobs could be threatened, or it could be their plan A. When I first was introduced to this industry, I had no idea how big my business could become. Not only did my monthly checks grow to what some people make in a year, but my whole lifestyle changed. I had earned the freedom to work and live as I dreamed. I could live in the right area; be there to watch my children's games; see them off to school. Even travel to where I wanted to go. It gave me security that no job could ever give.

I find the people who get into network marketing are often positive, like-minded people. You get to choose who you want to work with. What I never realized starting out was that some of those people have become lifelong friends, even family. The trips I have won, and my business trips will forever be in my memory as some of the best of times. Everyone has a dream, and they get to choose whether to act on it or not.

My question to you is, what if you never tried and never discovered your potential???

Sylvain Dion, CANADA

What put you in a situation where you wanted to start your own business through MLM?
At the time, I was in customer service for a courier company. I got injured and found myself off work with no income and unable to work. I had no other source of income and had just bought a new house. Stressed-out and not knowing how to cope, I was told about a product and a company that could help me, but I was skeptical. After trying everything else for my health problem, I took this product and the results were remarkable. That's when I decided to build my business in MLM.

What obstacle(s) have you overcome since the beginning of your MLM journey?
I believe that MLM is an endless pilgrimage and that if we stay in action, we will constantly evolve and become who we are called to become. The list of obstacles would be long if I listed them all. I believe that one of the greatest obstacles has been the fear of looking bad and not being up to the task. I can confirm to you that this fear needed to be addressed and that today this fear has been overcome by a spirit of courage and daring.

What is the best advice you have received since joining?
Never give up, and always continue to evolve with passion and conviction. Always remember that we have to be teachable, because the

day we forget that is the day we will start to experience a decline. We will no longer be able to give the right advice to other people who need it because we will have created our own plateau.

Why do you think everyone should consider MLM as a multiple source of income?

In the world we live in, there is no such thing as job security. More and more, we are slaves to the system, and it is becoming unreasonable to believe that by working for a linear wage we can achieve freedom. All the people I work with generally experience frustration and are not able to live without their paycheque. This is the importance of creating different sources of income, and one of these is through MLM, because it allows you to receive recurring residual income and thus have money to invest in your business and in other vehicles such as the stock market, real estate, etc.

Blanca Fernández, MEXICO

What originally put you in a situation where you wanted to build your own business via MLM?
What caught my attention was the opportunity to generate extra income, since my salary as a bank employee was not enough for me to be able to help my parents financially.

What obstacle(s) have you overcome since starting your MLM journey?
Since I started at a young age, the first obstacle I faced was credibility. When you are 16, 17, or 18 years old, you don't have a lot of credibility when it comes to speaking to adults.

The second obstacle I faced was time. I had two young children by the time I was 24 years old, and it was difficult to dedicate the time required. Especially since this business requires a LOT of training. As well, I didn't have the financial resources required for getting the level of training I needed.

Another obstacle was that my parents did not support my decision to get into this business. Instead, they would tell me to get a JOB. I had to learn to face criticism and not let it affect me.

Another obstacle came after my first divorce. To make the situation even more difficult, my daughter chose to live with her dad when the judge gave her the choice with whom to live. This was a very big blow to me.

Moving to a new city and leaving home, family, and friends felt like I was starting at the bottom because I felt alone with my son in a city where I didn't know anyone.

The second time I moved, it was to the capital of Mexico, a city that has different customs as well as a different dialect than I was used to. I found this to be a barrier that prevented me from relating to other people.

After my second divorce from a marriage where I suffered physical, psychological, and emotional aggression, I also went through a difficult time. Regardless, I dedicated myself for close to ten years to building a business with another company that I truly loved. Then I discovered that many of the products that I represented were also available for purchase in stores at a lower price than what I was allowed to sell them at. A good example is one product that was priced at $30 in my catalogue, but which was available for $6 in retail stores. Both had the same packaging but were labeled under a different brand.

Another obstacle I faced occurred when I started building my current business with the company I am with now. I didn't pay the monthly mortgage on my house, and within three months I almost lost my house, which was the only property I had.

Meanwhile I continued to help people develop by giving them my time and strategies for building a successful business. That said, I feel that the key to my success has been tolerance and an ability to manage frustration.

What is the best piece of advice you've received since joining?

What is priceless is not always appreciated. I understood from the beginning that succeeding in network marketing is not a business of speed but of persistence.

Why do you believe everyone should consider MLM as a multiple source of income?

Because MLM is the only business model that I know of that allows you to have a professional title and where you can transform the lives of many people, including your own. It also provides you with a capacity to earn an unimagined income while at the same time being a father and mother.

Ron Forrester and Leslie Hocker, USA

What originally put you in a situation where you wanted to build your own business via MLM?
My formal education is as a pharmacist, PharmD, and I had been out of school for seven years and working for a national chain when my boss gave me a "promotion." It was only later that I figured out that it wasn't a promotion at all. (No other idiot would do the job!)

I became the "rover" and covered all the other locations in a three-hour radius from my home. My boss would call me at 6:00 a.m. and tell me where he wanted me that day by 9 a.m., which could be anywhere within that three-hour-drive radius. So, I worked when other pharmacists were sick, on vacation, or any other reason someone would suddenly need the day off.

I would work from 11 to 14 hours for that day, depending on when the location closed. Often, I would overnight, too, and do the same the next day. I was working an average of 77 hours a week, not including my driving time. Add my driving time and I was easily "on the job" for 100 hours or so a week. The company was paying me reallllllllly well, even buying my toothpaste, per diem, mileage and many bonuses. I did it for 18 months without a day off. Not. One. Single. Day. Seven days a week.

I had two daughters, three and five years old, and I never saw them awake. At about 14 months into this, the mother of my children said to me, "You need to rethink this job. Your children don't even know you. Oh, and while you're rethinking it, think of getting something that pays the same."

I looked at everything, even multiple kiosks in malls. I became a "serial business-in-a-box" buyer from *Entrepreneur* Magazine. Nothing would do what my wife mentioned for me to think about.

For seven years prior to that, my next-door neighbor had been trying to get me to look at his "home business." And telling me it would make me rich. I paid no attention to him, because when he started talking to me, I knew I was being paid four times more than him. He was a city employee, and therefore his salary was public information. In 1972 he was making $12,500. I was making $50,000. During those years, my salary was going up, and the last two years it quadrupled. So, I wasn't listening to him.

BUT my time came. At about 18 months into that "promotion," I opened the Sunday newspaper for that little town, and the entire second page was on my next-door neighbor. It read, "(My neighbor) completes the largest real estate transaction in our history!"

He had gone up on the local mountain (a hill by most standards) and bought a brand-new mansion, and then went next door and bought another one, which he gave to his mother-in-law! I was blown away, to say the least.

I went to see him and asked him three questions (which I have learned are the universal questions every prospect is asking, even if only in their mind): 1. What do I really have to do? 2. How much time do I really have to spend doing that? 3. Can I really be expected to make an extra $500 in five or six months from now?

His answers to me were factual, and he made me think on several of them with his questions back to me. Sometimes, it would be a good thing for me to share those questions, answers, and back questions. I have learned that every prospect has the same ones!

As soon as I was satisfied with the answers, a team of horses could not have stopped me. I started working five hours a week on my business right then. To get the time, I totally gave up on any TV. The rest is history.

What obstacle(s) have you overcome since starting your MLM journey?

I am an introvert. Possibly the biggest introvert you have ever met! I came face-to-face with this fact when I was in the spring semester of my 10th grade in high school.

Let me set the stage. I grew up blessed with parents that loved me, blessed with the fact that I didn't lack for food or for clothing. But we were poor tenant farmers for a dentist who owned the beef farm in NC. (I found out when I moved to Texas that I didn't grow up on a "farm." That it was really a "ranch"—but that's another story.)

We had plenty of food, animals, fowl, and produce from our two-acre garden. (Which is huge, by the way! Try taking care of two acres of garden someday!) And we always canned and froze for the winter months.

Back to me being an introvert. Because we were tenant farmers and I was shy and introverted, I had a low self-image. As a result, I didn't "run" with a clique, so to speak, but I knew most everyone's name (the advantage of growing up in a small school; 472 total students). So, being the introvert, I didn't interact very much and avoided it as much as possible.

My lesson came on April 17, 1963, at approximately 11:00 a.m. I was coming out of the gymnasium and headed for a short 200-foot sidewalk that "T'd" into another that led to the high school to the left and the elementary school to the right. I get about 30 feet out of the gym—sidewalk was empty, which was nirvana for me—and down the big set of entrance steps at the high school skips the most beautiful girl in school. Blond. Blue eyes. Head cheerleader. Drum majorette. She was the one everyone lusted after, including me! I am in a pickle! Things are running through my mind fast. "Can I just turn around and go back inside? Nope, too far out. What can I say? Hi? No, that's dumb.

Hello? Oh, my goodness! That won't work!" My head was spinning, and it all got taken away from me in about 40 seconds. I can tell you how blue the sky was that day. I can still smell the fresh-cut grass around me. I can hear the kids playing on the swings in the playground over my left shoulder. I can tell you what I was wearing, and I can tell you what she was wearing. But I can't tell you what I said back to her when she said to me, "Hello, stuck-up!"

I was floored! My body was in school the rest of that day, but my mind was not. I was thinking, "These people think you are stuck up." But really, I wasn't. I was just scared to death! And then I thought, "You have got to do something that pulls you out of this shell or you will have a miserable life! You have to!"

I went through so many options that day, and when I did get out of class I went straight to the local teen hamburger hangout and got myself a job as a curb hop. I had reasoned if I did that, I would have to be of service and have to communicate and would learn how to socially interact.

It worked. I hated it, but I still did it and did it and did it. Eventually there was not one kid that I did not know, and at the end of my 11th grade (one year later) a good friend of mine was running for senior class president, but he came to me and told me that

I should run and that he thought I would win. I did, and it helped me get into my chosen university.

It also helped me talk to people and not be afraid to approach people, which is what you have to do in this profession! It turns out that was the single best social interaction for my personal growth I have ever had. It inspired me to do all I could to become a better person.

What is the best piece of advice you've received since joining?

Never quit. I have been in personal development since I was a pre-teen. My mom and my dad both developed a sense of responsibility in all of us (we were four kids), and it mostly boiled down to you could do anything you believed you could do. To persevere until the job was complete. When I joined the network marketing industry, I asked if it was reasonable to expect to make $500 a month extra after five or six months working five hours a week. The answer was yes; doesn't matter what happens along the way, just don't quit.

Sure, I've received many no's, but every time I took my clothes off at night, there was no blood. So, no's don't matter, and I didn't quit. Almost five months to the day later I had a check in my hands for $500. I remember looking at that check and making the most important decision of my life. I consider it the single most important decision because it led to all the great experiences of my life. I looked at that check and said to myself, "This works, contrary to what so many others say, and I'm going to stick around and see how far I can take it."

It's taken me pretty far! I once had a compliment from you, John, that you probably don't remember, but I do. We were in Clearbrook at our first National Marketing Director meeting and they were handing out all the awards for really just doing good business, which is what it boils down to. They handed out seven awards. I took six of them (should have had the seventh too, but politics stepped in and they gave the Leadership Award to a newbie in the company—accomplished in the business but not the company). Anyway, you were sitting behind me and tapped me on the shoulder and said, "I didn't know you were that good!"

You inspired me! I have held myself to the same high standards my entire career.

Why do you believe everyone should consider MLM as a multiple source of income?

By 1980, when I entered this business model, I had done a lot of thinking, and I believe if I had really been smart, instead of relying on my book learning and education, I would have gone into insurance sales right out of high school because that model uses the same wealth principles we do in this model (probably copied from the insurance model) of compounding, leveraging, and residual income. We do the same as the broker does that hires many agents and trains them to go sell the product, and he gets a small cut of many sales. We do the same as the apartment complex owner—set many streams of income in place, and if one is interrupted (someone quits), the other streams are still sending small amounts into the pot. Of course, to have those multiple people set up to send those many small streams, we pay a price. We travel, train, reward, work on weekends, and nights when others won't.

It took the man that recruited me seven years to get my interest and convince me. I have kicked myself many times for waiting those seven years. If everyone out there really understood the power of leveraging, compounding, and residual income, a different environment would exist today. Everyone should have multiple streams of income in case something happens to one of them.

Using money as a measure only, I know in my case exactly what the difference is. My raise when I worked in pharmacy was capped at 3% a year. I calculated my total income over 40 years of doing that at a 3% increase per year and believe me when I say that I have made more, twelve times more, in my Relationship Marketing career vs Doctor of Pharmacy career. But that is not the real compensation. The real compensation is the people I have helped to change their lives for the positive! Imagine the legacy you and I have! This is part of the wonderful compensation of this model. We will have big legacies. Many people will remember how much we helped them and in so many ways. And in both our cases the income from the marketing model has afforded us the chance to do outreach programs that have directly impacted the lives of others, millions of others now. That is a legacy very few get to leave!

I am extremely honored that you asked me to participate in this book because maybe, just maybe, someone will read one of my stories and it will be the start of something new and big for them. You keep taking those big steps, my man. I'm right there with you!

Robin Francis, TRINIDAD AND TOBAGO

What originally put you in a situation where you wanted to build your own business via MLM?
I was married to one of the most beautiful ladies in the world, and I wanted to give her the best life I could. After going to a presentation, I realized that only MLM could have afforded me the opportunity to do so without a doctorate or law licence.

What obstacle(s) have you overcome since starting your MLM journey?
Being stuck in a job with fixed wages.

No money to travel all over the world to explore and enjoy my life.

Having a certain level of financial freedom to support my family.

The obstacle of working hard instead of working smart.

What is the best piece of advice you've received since joining?
The secret to success is simple: talk to a lot of people.

The business is not about me; it's about helping others get what they want in life through my business.

Why do you believe everyone should consider MLM as a multiple source of income?

MLM is getting 1% of 100 people's effort rather than getting 100% of your own effort.

This is the best method for earning income, because if one day you find yourself in a situation where you can't work, you can still earn an income because it's not based solely on your own effort.

Joe Garcia, CANADA

What originally put you in a situation where you wanted to build your own MLM business?
After the fitness/racquet club I was managing was sold during the Christmas season in 1992, I realized I was building someone else's dream instead of mine. I promised myself then that I would never work for someone else again.

A few months later I did not know what came over me, but I decided that I would spend an hour planning my next ten years, writing down what I wanted to achieve. The first three things on the list were 1) I knew the key to a great lifestyle was to earn money while you slept (residual income). 2) I had just become a dad for the first time and my dream was to spend as much time with my son as I could, so working from home was a must (even though I did not know anyone that worked from home at the time). 3) Since I was going to work from home, I desperately wanted a DREAM HOME.

As soon as I wrote this vision, I fell in love with it. It became my purpose, and every day it played in the movie of my mind multiple times daily.

About eight weeks later I was in my local library studying types of businesses, and a gentleman walked up to me and introduced me to network marketing. He did such a poor job following up, and it took him 30 days to book an appointment with me. It was the worst business presentation I had ever seen. I came home after the meeting still not impressed. Again, his follow-up was poor. A few weeks later he introduced me to his upline and invited me to meet with him. His upline pulled out a check for $3,500 for the month. This was his fifth month in the business. Now it got my attention. I was then invited to a Super-Saturday event, and within a few minutes after the start of the meeting, my body was on fire from head to toe and I knew from every part of myself that this was going to be my vehicle to my DREAMS.

This is when I learned that when you fall in love with your DREAM, the universe will conspire to get you what you want. The random library connection, as I look back all these years later, is something that I manifested as soon as I fell in love with my DREAM.

What obstacles have you overcome since starting your MLM journey?

The main obstacle I had to overcome was myself. The beliefs I had about myself created obstacles that hurt my self-esteem, and I compared myself to others. Through personal development every day, and acting on my business every day, the consistency grew my conscious level and I realized these thoughts were not real and that they were programmed into me.

We are all made up from the same source. When I reflected on this, I realized that God does not make junk. I connected to the power we all have inside of us, and this made me unstoppable.

What is the best piece of advice you've received since joining?

Through my personal development journey, which included all the books I read, I came to realize that all the wisdom in the world comes down to one thing: We are the masters of our destiny. Remember when you first fell in love and how you didn't have to remind yourself to think about that person because they were always playing in the movie of your mind? Well, when we fall in love with our DREAM, which needs to be very specific, in God's perfect wisdom the universe conspires for us until we manifest it. This is the #1 law of the universe.

Why do you believe everyone should consider MLM as a multiple source of income?
A few years ago, I attended a seminar, and one of the speakers was a professor of business at the University of Germany. He shocked the audience when he stated, "In the next twenty years, about 90% of the jobs today will disappear due to technology." We all know that technology will create new jobs, but we don't know if it will keep up with the number of jobs that are lost. Whether he was correct or not, we have seen this trend happen during our lifetime. It's only smart financial planning to have a plan B in your life.

Jamie Hawley, CANADA

What originally put you in a situation where you wanted to build your own business via MLM?
I taught school in Canada, earning a very good income, BUT throughout my career I really wanted to be my own boss. With several years to go before retirement at age 47, I decided to exit teaching to pursue something on my own. I had a substantial pension built, and to access some of that sweat equity I moved my pension to where I could access some of it. The person I trusted with my entire life proved to be a thief, stealing the entire $750,000.00 I was in total shock!!

What obstacle(s) have you overcome since starting your MLM journey?
Due to the theft of my only financial asset, I ended up having to go on social assistance, which was a meager $400.00 per month. I had to find a way to make money, and when I was presented with the opportunity to investigate an MLM company by Wally Kralik, I jumped at the chance in spite of having no experience in sales and certainly none in MLM. During my 23 years in the same company, I have earned a very good income and have had the best years of my working life.

What is the best piece of advice you've received since joining?
Wally always drills in the idea of focusing on what you want and doing only those actions that will help you attain your goals.

Be positive, be consistent, and treat this like a business, not a hobby.

Why do you believe everyone should consider MLM as a multiple source of income?
The key word here for me to stress to anyone looking at our industry is "freedom." Especially with my company's product line, pay plan, and timing in the marketplace, this is a business where one can realistically look at earning a very solid part-time income. And for those who are willing to learn and spend the time and effort, a nice full-time income is very realistic. Why not work hard for 4 to 5 years with an MLM company that you believe in and become financially stable rather than giving your life up to a corporation for the next 39 to 40 years (if you are fortunate enough to get a good JOB), only to have them cut you loose in the end with perhaps nothing but a small pension, too small to do the things you now want to do in retirement?

Network marketing is the only way to achieve freedom on your terms while enjoying what you do.

Keith Hooper, USA

What originally put you in a situation where you wanted to build your own business via MLM?
I had 140+ employees and no free time.

What obstacle(s) have you overcome since starting your MLM journey?
Not understanding how someone can hate their life and still not want to look at MLM.

What is the best piece of advice you've received since joining?
Learning to leverage the uplines.

Why do you believe everyone should consider MLM as a multiple source of income?
The times we live in are such that uncertainty is around every corner.

Patricia Karalash, CANADA

What originally put you in a situation where you wanted to build your own business via MLM?
I am a prairie farmer's daughter. I love nature and animals. When I retired after 33 years as a registered nurse working in critical care departments, I never imagined I would discover a product that would save my health. I felt really good. I was back out walking my dogs for the first time in two years. My friends and neighbors wanted to know what happened and why I looked so good! They said the same thing to me as I said to my girlfriend who introduced me to the life-changing product: "Get me some?"

That's how I began my fast-track to networking and direct sales that has helped me to change my life and the lives of others. It is a natural extension of my passion to help the world and be who I was born to be.

What obstacles have you overcome since starting your MLM journey?
Learning how to talk to others so my information is meaningful and so that they can make informed decisions which has meant classes, courses, and meetings.

Wow! Has my brain expanded!

Why do you believe everyone should consider MLM or multiple source of income?

Everyone should consider MLM because you are supported by many. You get what you put in, BUT you have this entire team behind you that WANTS to help you in any way they can. How many jobs can you say that about? In MLM I've been helped by extraordinary and talented people that I otherwise would never have met. As a result, I have formed incredible relationships. I am blessed.

It's an exciting world out there!

Lou Kokkinakos, USA

What originally put you in a situation where you wanted to build your own business via MLM?
The tale of two friends. I have been friends with John Solleder for over twenty years and have watched him create a very successful business in network marketing just as I have created a very successful business in the entertainment industry. While my business grew, I continued to work longer and harder days.

Meanwhile, every time I spoke with John, he was at one of his children's events. I knew I needed to start working toward building a residual income with the ability to have the time freedom that John has.

The push to finally build this came as the coronavirus hit. Again, I have a thriving business, but because of the national emergency and social distancing situation, within 24 hours I had over $60k in business cancelled, and there was nothing I could do about it. This is when I realized that I can no longer leave anything to chance; I need to build a residual income.

What obstacle(s) have you overcome since starting your MLM journey?
With my busy schedule, finding the time to get this off the ground and do the research to apply the marketing techniques I've learned in the entertainment industry to MLM.

Why do you believe everyone should consider MLM as a multiple source of income?

In recent days, we have quickly learned that it's not business as usual anymore. So many industries have been affected to a point where, like me, we are losing income for an indefinite period, and it's very stressful. To create a multiple source of income would provide times like these with an insurance policy for not struggling and prospering instead.

Arlene Lowy, USA

What originally put you in a situation where you wanted to build your own business via MLM?
During my late 20s I was disgusted to work absurd hours and develop more business for a company that paid me the same salary of $36,000 a year. By complete luck, I was dating a fellow who threw a box in the middle of the table and introduced me to Herbalife. I loved that I could create a secondary income and help people both lose weight and create additional money. That was all I needed to walk into my boss's office and say I am leaving. Yes, they tried to throw incentives at me, but it was too late. I was not afraid because I always was an A-type personality and overworked.

Everything about this business was so attractive to me, and I saw the word freedom written in capital letters. Looking back over the last 35 years, I made the best decision, and now instead of being paralyzed during a pandemic, I am financially sound and can help others get through this trying time.

What obstacle(s) have you overcome since starting your MLM journey?
I became a single mom early on in the business and had to learn to juggle my son's life and mine. I felt guilty that I could not attend all his events and really gave up a lot, but he became my best student.

He saw me be at high income levels while companies were going under, and more than once he watched me start all over. I have watched him pick up the best of my strengths and soar in whatever he decides to partake in.

What is the best piece of advice you've received since joining?

The best advice is this is a great industry that is affordable to become a part of. You can start part-time and create a secondary income that sometimes exceeds your primary income. You can touch so many lives with great products and introduce them to financial freedom. You can own your life and design it the way you want it to be.

Why do you believe everyone should consider MLM as a multiple source of income?

There is absolutely no business out there that is this rewarding in helping others and having a lifestyle that affords freedom no matter what is happening in the world. Residual income was so important for me to learn about. I did not mind overworking to get highly overpaid. I had already put those hours in for others. I love that I design every day for myself and my family. I do not answer to anyone but myself.

Susy Lozano, MEXICO

What put you in a situation where you wanted to build your own business through network marketing?

At one stage in my life, after my divorce, I was presented with two options to generate income. The first was to be part of a company as a distributor, and the second option was to work as an employee behind a desk and conform with a salary. I thought it was the "safest" choice since it would allow me to have a fixed monthly income. So, I chose this option and worked in that company, depending on the vice presidency for several years.

I was excited because I gained experience and knowledge as the company grew and expanded its borders. However, the years went by and I was still in the same position in my company, behind the desk. Yet others advanced. Since I wanted to move up in life, this helped me make the decision to become an entrepreneur.

One of the things I noticed was that the people that joined network marketing remarkably improved their leadership, their income, and their social and family life. This was yet another defining moment for me to make the decision to start my own business. It is true that the lack of experience in MLM caused me fear; however, I did not start from scratch, since I already had the knowledge that I acquired by working as a staff member in the aforementioned company. I also had the confidence of people who knew me, and that's why they invited me to partner with them in network marketing.

For many years I would say that the decision to be employed had been a mistake. Today, thank God, I see things differently. I appreciate having worked as an employee since I was in a place where I learned about administration, sales, and finance, among other things. It also increased my capacity for analysis, observation, and decision-making. Something very important was meeting many people who have been great teachers of life for me. For this reason, I can say that each decision we make in life, we do it thinking that it is the right thing to do, since each experience gives us the opportunity to learn, grow, mature, and improve. Today I know that I would not be the same without the experience gained in my job as an employee.

What obstacles have you overcome since joining network marketing?

Analyzing the situations that I have experienced in network marketing, I can say that they haven't been obstacles, difficulties, barriers, or limitations. I consider myself fortunate and abundantly blessed by God. People have honored me with their trust and help, and I have a son who has always understood and supported me for the countless hours and days in which I had to be absent to work and give him a better quality of life.

I have to say that being away from home for work has been one of the biggest challenges I have had to live, since it is difficult to fulfill my obligations as a mother, daughter, sister, and a friend when you have commitments, goals, and personal longings and that of a team that believes in you. However, I was able to get ahead and spend time with my son, my family, my business, and friends.

I can say that in network marketing, more than obstacles, I have had many challenges. Just to name a few, I will tell you that being an entrepreneur and your own boss entails increasing your responsibility and commitment. You must grow your talents and develop communication, managerial, leadership, and negotiation skills, among others.

Other challenges are organizing and taking advantage of time, constant updating, continuous improvement, teamwork, strengthening your network and, above all, not losing your values but improving them. Trust yourself more, both in your business and in the company you represent and to which you belong. These values are the result of living in consistency and continuous improvement.

What is the best advice you have received since you started?

First of all, I want to thank God for giving me great teachers that have dedicated time to me.

I am convinced that one of the best pieces of advice I received was to believe in myself. Because of starting this business at the age of 50, which was not easy in the beginning, I learned that age does not determine how you live life, nor does it determine the success or failure of your projects.

Today I would give you the same advice. Believe in yourself and do not forget your essence of being human; respect each person with whom you live; support and help your work teams—be a good example for them. Base your work on the values of faith, trust, respect, loyalty, honesty, solidarity, harmony, and love.

Work with balance, conviction, and consistency; be generous and grateful. Strengthen your business as you help your associates achieve their goals and achieve their dreams. Set goals that challenge you, train and be open to learning. Do not lose your simplicity; be happy and look for others to be.

Dan McCormick, USA

What originally put you in a situation where you wanted to build your own business via MLM?
A dream of freedom. I wasn't qualified to do anything else after finishing college!

What obstacle(s) have you overcome since starting your MLM journey?
Woefully immature! It took seven years of working on me every day before I trusted the process.

What is the best piece of advice you've received since joining?
Learning to enjoy the journey and approach every day with a genuine interest in helping others!

Why do you believe everyone should consider MLM as a multiple source of income?
Well, not sure I would. But if you're dissatisfied, then you have every reason to look, learn, leap! It has every possibility of changing your life for the better. While at the same time giving you the opportunity to serve others, which is the greatest reward we can get.

Jeffrey McTavish, UK

What originally put you in a situation where you wanted to build your own business via MLM?
My original exposure to MLM products and opportunity was back in the 1980s.

However, I did not take heed to the business that was presented, as I was too busy raising a young family and had a busy family business, both of which took all my attention and energy.

Then in the early '90s I found myself in a different situation and met someone in a retail environment who had a badge on his lapel that I recognized from the '80s and inquired about what it was representing. I remember the meeting that followed and the excitement that was attached with it. I wanted to be a part of this opportunity; however, the person who wore that badge lived many, many miles away and did not mentor me to take advantage of the business opportunity that was being offered. I needed the opportunity for the income that it could potentially give me as well as the personal growth that comes with this industry.

I was not ready to hear such a call. Fast-forward several years and I live in a different country, while I am embarking on a new career that was to be my future life. I rejoined the same company that I was associated with whilst living in a different country and tried to "do the business," but I found that I was not ready; my spirit had other priorities for my future.

I graduated in the profession of the true design of whom I was destined to be. In the midst of my studies I had experimented with various direct selling companies, but the coat did not fit me. As I moved through my new professional career, I was exposed to various network marketing companies because the product resonated with who I am and what I do for my livelihood. The business plan was secondary.

This all changed when I found that the elements of right time, right product, right environment, and right need became important to my personal and professional persona. All the frequencies of product, commitment, science, and a sound, strong business acumen to build a secondary income melded in one company that made sense to me.

What obstacle(s) have you overcome since starting your MLM journey?

There were many obstacles in my experience with my involvement in MLM companies.

The most prevalent obstacle that blocked me from the many opportunities was believing in myself; that I could be successful and be able to have the self-acceptance to deserve the success that was on offer. I would say that the biggest block was MYSELF. However, when purpose meets opportunity in the guise of a product and business that enhance how you define yourself and your beliefs, then that opportunity and product/service becomes a purpose that resonates with who you are. There are no obstacles, for the alignment of the outcome of the product/service becomes an extension of you and your values. The puzzle of completion that has eluded you with many different pieces finds the right fit. The picture becomes clear and you are no longer the one who holds back the opportunity to be that piece which helps complete our life's picture for those to see on your wall of life.

What is the best piece of advice you've received since joining?

They say that the student is ready when the right teacher comes around. Time has a plan of its own. It's all about having ears to hear and being in a state of a student, ready to learn and not try to reinvent the wheel.

KISS—keep it simple, and TEAM—together everyone achieves more. These are the best acronyms for life.

This is what took 20 years of my life to hear. My ears were filled with ego and professional stubbornness and ignorance. Once I had seen through the veil of this futility and had my brain syringed with reality, the student was ready, and the right teachers were there at the right time for me to listen to them.

The advice and guidance of us all, no matter your career, is to learn from those that inspire you, whatever avenue you choose to walk down. Be open to constructive criticism and cast aside all ego and all preconceptions of what you know. There is always someone that will know more than you; just accept that this is a reality and that the road of knowledge opens from a single lane to a vast motorway. Couple this with an ego-ectomy of you, your "self," and the road will lead you to many riches, both personal, spiritual, and financial.

Why do you believe everyone should consider MLM as a multiple source of income?

The question has been asked, "Why would anyone believe or consider getting involved in a direct selling adventure?"

Based on my personal experience, there are many, many reasons to pursue this business adventure. For most people, it is a venue to supplement an income that they work hard for or that does not fulfill the financial requirement of their needs.

However, to follow this path with a product or service that does not resonate with you and your core being will ultimately fail. The substance and validity of the opportunity and your inner desire and passion will have a short life. In order to light the candle of desire so that we may see your light, is to Be the many flickers of flame that attempts to be the bearer of ignition, for that ultimate spark which will light your fire. When flame meets the wick, the candle will burn, and when all elements are one in which no wind of discontentedness or admonishment that breeds self-doubt or ridicule upon your favor, are only to be extinguished be your beacon of an undeniable restitution of your resolve to bring your business, your product, to the lives you touch.

Rolando Rivera Moreno, MEXICO–
English and Spanish

What put you in a situation where you wanted to build your own business through network marketing?
An economic bankruptcy and urgency to recover my stability.

What obstacles have you overcome since you started your career in network marketing?
I had two obstacles. The first obstacle was not believing in the industry, the company, and its magnitude. The second obstacle was the fear of speaking with people that I didn't know.

What is the best advice you have received since you started?
Learn quickly and follow the instructions.

Why do you think everyone should consider network marketing as an option to receive additional income?
Because it's all about connecting with people who need to solve something with people or products that solve it.

Marco Navarro, MEXICO

What originally put you in a situation where you wanted to build your own business via MLM?
Definitely, what put me in the situation of making a decision to want something different and reach network marketing was that burning desire to realize my dreams, to live well. Also, of course, being inside the business, I realized that I could help many others. Basically, I made the decision, as the great dreamer that I am, believing faithfully that it was the opportunity that I was already waiting for to be able to live differently and be free as I am nowadays. Something else that led me to the network marketing industry was that search for my financial freedom, because of a situation at the age of thirty-five which I did not want to see myself in at the age of seventy or more, if I lived that long: in precarious conditions, carrying cardboard or with my outstretched hand asking for alms, because my economic situation was not good, since my studies were only elementary school and my profession was that of a carpenter. I knew that if I continued with my beliefs and the lifestyle I had, my life would end very badly.

What obstacle(s) have you overcome since starting your MLM journey?
The first one was to realize that EVERYTHING depended on me. That success is not just about high quality or the company or about

a good partner. It is not just about a good product or a good compensation plan. It is mainly about the decisions that one makes, in the determination and character that is forged in order to get ahead and find oneself and confront oneself. The most important challenges are precisely the realization that I had to follow a system, that I had to be teachable. That was hard for me. To break with the arrogance of believing that I knew everything, when in reality I knew nothing. At that time, I learned that network marketing is a profession and that I had to do it professionally. I learned that I had to let myself be taught by others. It would be needless to tell you how many people said no to me. Of course, with a little perseverance, believing in yourself and defending your dreams, you can overcome that. That is the daily part of it. Learning to receive NO. That was no problem for me, because when I decided, those NO's didn't matter. What mattered to me were my dreams, and what I found was that I had to educate Marco, I had to train him, I had to develop him and help him discover what he was capable of. The most important challenge was to believe in myself.

What is the best piece of advice you've received since joining?

I don't have one in particular. I've received a lot of good advice along the way that has been fundamental and with the same level of importance. The first was that my sponsor, Javier Rayas, gave me a book and said, "Get to read." That meant: "Get ready." When I said, "I want to be a leader," he gave me a book and said, "Read the first chapter," and he gave me a second lesson, because he said, "Prepare a topic with it, and you are going to teach the training."

So, for me there were two very powerful messages: One, get trained, educate yourself; and the second, put it into practice, don't keep it to yourself. I have understood that knowledge is rubbish when we just accumulate it without putting it into action. It is like faith, which many think is about believing and nothing else. No. To believe is to believe, period. It is hoping for something without doing anything. And everyone believes, but not everyone has faith. For me, it is very clear. Faith is the certainty of what is going to happen, but it goes further. That is why it says in the book of James that faith without work is not faith. From this I understood that faith must be accompanied by actions, by being consistent, leading by example, moving forward. And those things are the most valuable for the fundamental foundation to my success.

Why do you believe everyone should consider MLM as a multiple source of income?

Consider network marketing as an option? I think we are wrong. IT IS NOT AN OPTION! Network marketing today is a reality. It is an urgent need, and I simply want to convey what my concept of network marketing is. It's just about connecting people and helping them discover themselves as people that have the right to live in prosperity and freedom. We are free human beings whom the network marketing profession allows, precisely, to make decisions, when we want, how we want them, and where we want. But the most important thing is to understand that IT IS NOT AN OPTION. It is an urgent need. I don't know if you want to wait until you have to do it because you no longer have any other options, since right now it seems that you have an apparent advantage of choosing a job.

But today more than ever we are aware that jobs are going to disappear and that they are disappearing by millions after the situation we are experiencing with the pandemic, and that the best way to earn an income is very simple.

Why network marketing? Because it's about making a partnership with the greats, and by partnering with the greats and learning from them, you're definitely going to be successful. There's no more! Whatever I could tell you, I know others have already repeated that before. But for me it is not an option. It is the best opportunity that exists to be free and discover the human being that you are.

David Ogunnaike, AKA Super Dave, CANADA

What originally put you in a situation where you wanted to build your own MLM business?

I was almost $100k in debt, and I had finally decided I couldn't continue with just the job I was working at because it would never help me catch up on my bills and expenses.

Plus, half of my debt was co-signed with my mom and she wanted to retire, and she couldn't as long as she had this debt hovering over her.

So that was the push that made me get serious about building my MLM business.

What obstacles have you overcome since starting your MLM journey?

How many do you want? :-)

- First, family members will not always be as supportive as you would like.
- Prospects will tell you what you want to hear but will not follow through or will join the witness protection program.
- Driving 8+ hours to meet a prospect and they don't show up or flying to launch a city and the main person that invited you cancels after you land at the airport.

- Company owners stop paying me my commission.
- Companies just shut down.

What is the best piece of advice you've received since joining?

The best piece of advice I ever got was to always stay at a number 5 regardless of what someone says or what is happening around you.

For example, when you meet a prospect and they say that they are so excited, and they will be your biggest leader. They are a 10 on a scale of 1 to 10. You just stay at a 5.

And the next day when you call them to get started, they say they spoke to their broke brother-in-law, and now they are not interested. So now they are a 0 on the 1 to 10 scale (they don't even make it to 1). Guess what? You just stay at a 5.

This way you are able to control your emotions and are not easily swayed one way or the other.

Why do you believe everyone should consider MLM as a multiple source of income?

I think today it's easier than ever to get involved with an MLM company.

It's the simplest way for someone to get started with a business from home.

Plus, if you partner up with the right leader and company, then you will get access to training and skills that should make you a better person in everything you do in life.

Most of the people that come in for money with MLM, and those that commit, learn, and grow find that they do make that extra money, but they are also able to increase their income in anything else they are involved with.

Miriam Pfeil, UK

What originally put you in a situation where you wanted to build your own business via MLM?

Back in 2016, I worked for the London Ambulance Service as an emergency medical technician. This job was my absolute dream career and it took me a long time, hard work, and commitment in order to get there. To this point, I lived a very stressful, unhealthy lifestyle doing shift work, being a student as well as a single parent. Sadly, I had to sacrifice on sleep, and this eventually triggered a hefty epileptic seizure which woke me up to reality on December 26, 2016.

My entire life changed! My dream of becoming a paramedic busted in four minutes.

From that day onwards, my career as an emergency medical technician changed into office administration. I had to undergo many hospital appointments and tests in order to figure out what triggered my brain to have a seizure.

In the meantime, I was grounded from the ambulance work and not allowed to drive regular cars or the emergency ambulances because the risk of having more seizures was extremely high. My driving licence had to be returned to the DVLA, which meant that I had to rely on public transportation for everything. I lived in Horsham and my employer was in New Malden, London. Talk about a bad day at the office.

At that time, I was a full-time student and working single mum with absolutely zero support from parents, grandparents, or the father of my son, who was 8 years old at that time. My commute to work changed from a 50-minute car ride to 2 hours by train. That's a 4-hour commute from Monday to Friday, 8 hours of office work, which I had absolutely no interest in, and a huge pay cut, plus spending 350 pounds more on train travel for my Oyster card. What a joke! I ended up spending more money on travel and childcare than I actually earned, plus I was very frustrated about the fact that I was not able to continue with my paramedic career.

Six months later I received the news from the hospital with the diagnosis of severe epilepsy. When I had the consultation with my neurologist, he recommended that I take strong medication to help eliminate future seizures. He told me that my second EEG looked severely abnormal and the chance of having more seizures was very high. I refused the medication because I knew that I would not be able to drive a car ever again. The news came as a real shock to me, and my entire dream of becoming a paramedic burst when I read the email and met my doctor! How could I be epileptic after having just one big seizure? Then I remembered. When I was 14 years old, I had electrodes of an EEG on my head. I must have had a seizure then. Luckily, I cannot remember when I have them. I'm unconscious.

The NHS and my boss were really supportive and created this new office role for me, which I took on for 9 months. The travel and extra cost made it really difficult for me and my son to sustain a living. I was worse off than before and really unhappy. I knew that I had to wait for a minimum of 5 years until I could get my C1 driving licence and 1 year until I got my regular car driving licence back—provided I stayed seizure-free. There was no guarantee that I could still become a paramedic. I was broke and lost.

After many sleepless nights of figuring out what the best solution would be, I decided to start my own mindfulness business from home and left the Ambulance Service in October 2017.

So that is what I did. I felt a great relief, and I knew that I had made the right decision. I wanted to spend more time with my son, feel better, live a more fulfilled life, and most importantly, I wanted us to both be happy. I started working on myself. I went on courses, practised mindfulness in the form of meditation almost every day, started my own meditation classes and psychic development circle, changed my sleep pattern, ate better, removed toxins from my diet, and removed toxic relations as well. Life was good again.

I created a new vision board of what I truly wanted. One of the most important things that I wanted was a healthy brain!!! As well as an amazing job that would allow me to work part-time from home, earn an infinite amount of money, a truly happy and wonderful relationship with my soul mate, more children, a house on the beach, worldwide travel for my new family … the list still goes on.

I knew that I could reinvent my entire life by making decisions and taking the right actions based upon my heart's desires. Then it happened. The man from my vision board knocked on my door, literally. He had an appointment with me. To cut a long story short, we instantly became friends, and within four weeks this turned into the most beautiful relationship. He was a well-toned gentleman, a father of three beautiful girls, a Doctor of Chiropractic, musical, educated, and such a kindred spirit. He made me laugh, not cry. What a bonus! One of my biggest dreams became a reality. Then he introduced me to a wonderful product and MLM opportunity!

What obstacles have you overcome since starting your MLM journey?

Negativity and disbelief!

When I started sharing the product on a frequent basis, I met many open, positive-minded people as well as the complete opposite. I learned quickly that I needed to stop convincing people with a negative attitude and closed mindset toward the product or its business model. I realized that I could choose who I wanted to work with, so I started actively looking for positive, driven people who wanted to know all about the product and its potential. People with a dream and passion to build a successful business filled with happy, driven people.

Another obstacle was the fact that people misinterpret MLM and pyramid systems. Every person who works for someone is theoretically involved in a pyramid sales system.

What is the best advice you have been given since joining?

People like simple things! Keep it simple! Do not overwhelm them with too much information as they will start switching off halfway through the conversation, and eventually they will run away as they think that there must be something suspicious. We are not here to convince people; we are here to help people with their physical, mental, spiritual matters. We are here to help them to create a better lifestyle.

Why do you believe everyone should consider MLM as a multiple source of income?

Because this type of business can create freedom on all levels once it is established. You can earn an infinite amount of money if you wish to. You can choose who you are working with and where you would like to work. You can travel and take the business wherever you like and as far as you like. There are no limitations apart from the ones you set for yourself and others. You are the boss, and you can work on it whenever you feel like.

It's one of the most convenient ways of earning a sustainable income.

Carissa Rogers, USA

What originally put you in a situation where you wanted to build your own business via MLM?
Funnily enough, I started out just wanting to cover my car payment. I got approved for a car that I really couldn't afford. I quickly realized I could (more than) replace my income from my nine-to-five and turn it into a lucrative career. It was then when I hit rock bottom and I WOKE UP. I found myself working seven days a week: 8- to 10-hour days, not happy or fulfilled, and I was still broke. I took my three young kids to the store, and while I was there, I checked my bank account. That's when I realized that I was going to have to choose between buying milk for my two toddlers or cereal for my oldest son. That night I went home and cried for hours and prayed. I prayed a lot. That week, the perfect opportunity and mentor came into my life, changing my life forever. While it was hard at the time, it was probably the best thing to happen to me, because my life has never looked the same and I am so grateful.

What obstacle(s) have you overcome since starting your MLM journey?
Not caring what others think about me. I struggled with this a lot in the beginning. What I learned is that they will judge you anyway, so you may as well put yourself out there and go for your dreams. I

wanted time freedom, financial freedom, and to raise my own kids. I couldn't worry about what anyone thought of me. If I did, my dreams would have never come true.

What is the best piece of advice you've received since joining?
The best advice I have received that has really stuck with me ... is to be coachable. If someone has what you want, listen to them AND apply what you learn. Also, to not be attached to the outcome. Your best friend of twenty years or your Aunt Sally may think what you're doing is completely crazy or may not approve of you or this new life. Who cares? Someone will. And they will join you. Your warm market may not be the ones to help you reach your dreams, but just keep going. You WILL find them as long as you NEVER give up.

Why do you believe everyone should consider MLM as a multiple source of income?
MLM is a beautiful industry when you find the right products, compensation plan and culture, and people. Residual income is a beautiful thing. I for one realized that I needed to be earning money while I was asleep, or I would be working until the day I die. I chose not to trade my time for money, but rather to leverage my time and people. When I learned this at the age of 35, my whole world changed. And the future has never looked brighter.

Mariluz Sanchez, USA

What originally put you in a situation where you wanted to build your own business via MLM?
Starting a family was important to me and my husband and taking care of my babies was a priority. That meant sacrificing a good-paying job in the '90s, simplifying our lives, and moving to a smaller apartment with a rent we could afford. We had all our basic needs covered, but we had no savings, no emergency money. If we had to fix our car or an unexpected emergency came up, that meant delaying the payment of our bills. That meant more complications, because we had to pay late payment fees. If we were not careful, it would become "borrowing from Peter to pay Paul."

That's when we knew we needed an extra income. We were looking for something that would not interfere with our main goal, mom staying at home, taking care of her baby, but that we could have that extra $200 to $500 a month that could take care of the extras.

What obstacle(s) have you overcome since starting your MLM journey?
At the beginning of my journey with MLM, the toughest part was dealing with rejection. The cold market was terrifying to me. I was young and had no experience in the industry. I remember making

a list of people I wanted to approach. There was this lady who had an expensive car. She would smile at me every time we came across each other in the market or in the park. I thought I was warming up to her even though we had never had a conversation. And the one day I finally had the guts to approach her, instead of starting a friendship, I saw her with a $ sign. I just jumped her with a brochure in my hand. She surprised me with the loudest NO I've ever heard in my life. She rushed back to her car and never gave me another smile again.

I think about this now, and I can only look back and laugh at my inexperience. I cried a little and felt like a loser for a day. But I immediately understood my mistake. This was only the beginning of a learning process that would help me become a future leader.

What is the best piece of advice you've received since joining?
FOLLOWING THE GOLDEN RULE WILL ALWAYS BE A POSITIVE GUIDELINE.

Applying the Golden Rule means turning your attention to others, seeking out occasions to do good for those around you. It also means being outgoing and sincere, taking a personal interest in others.

Why do you believe everyone should consider MLM as a multiple source of income?
It has been proven time and time again that even in times of recession, MLM has pulled through. MLM for our family has meant freedom to do the things we love. Taking time to care for a loved one and still getting a paycheck in the mail. It meant getting a free car while in a hospital battling cancer while expecting a baby. It has

meant putting food on our table even in times of financial trouble. It was school for my three children. And it has given our family the opportunity to meet many wonderful people that we are proud to call our friends, and some, even our family.

Gian-Carlo Torres, USA

What originally put you in a situation where you wanted to build your own business via MLM?
I was 19 and BROKE! Becoming an entrepreneur was always a dream for me, and when I graduated from high school, owning a business was a goal. Now, there were two challenges. The first challenge was that I had NO money to start. The second challenge was that I HAD NO IDEA how to start! So, when I was first exposed to MLM and I understood that I only had to invest a couple of hundred dollars to start, without the headaches that a normal entrepreneur has, it was a WIN-WIN!

What obstacle(s) have you overcome since starting your MLM journey?
One big obstacle that I have overcome has been in DEALING WITH MY EMOTIONS. Entrepreneurship can be a very emotional ride, so in the beginning, I would react emotionally to everything. If someone said YES to my business, I was the happiest guy of the week. If someone said NO, I was the saddest guy of the week. This wasn't a good thing, because my emotions were so involved in everything that I wasn't consistent. When I started to control my emotions, everything started to change, because the way I started REACTING to problems started to change.

What is the best piece of advice you've received since joining?

To see FAILURE as a friend! Since I would see everything as a win-lose situation, then failing at something in business was a horrible thing for me. Once I TRULY learned that failure is a friend and that the goal is for me to learn from it, then that's when I started "failing forward."

Why do you believe everyone should consider MLM as a multiple source of income?

Because there isn't a better multiple-source-of-income opportunity! Nowadays, a lot of people would consider Uber/Lyft as a multiple source of income. While they aren't bad options, you should ask yourself: Does it give you leverage? Are you part of an important mission while driving other people? Can it help you earn full income on a part-time basis? Only MLM has these benefits. Best of all, MLM is really fun.

Mark Zuckerbrod, USA

What originally put you in a situation where you wanted to build your own business via MLM?
My biggest motivator was that I didn't want to work for someone else. I was willing to work very hard, but I hated being told what to do or that I had to be at a certain place at a certain time and do what a boss told me. That desire for time freedom and financial freedom really drove me. I started in this type of business at age 23 and it has given me the freedom to totally own and run my own life, which has been as valuable as the significant financial success my wife and I have had.

What obstacle(s) have you overcome since starting your MLM journey?
There have been many over the years, and the biggest initial one was learning to accept that when someone wasn't interested in my product or my business, it really had nothing to do with me. Also, in the early days we dealt with so many shipping issues, inventory issues, having to purchase everything by the case and distribute to our customers and team, etc. You had to be at a certain level even to purchase directly from the company. There was no drop shipping or auto ship to individual people, so everything was much more difficult and time-consuming. Those problems shouldn't exist anymore, but those early obstacles made us much stronger.

What is the best piece of advice you've received since joining?

I have received a few pieces of great advice over the years. Probably the most important is not to let someone telling you NO get you discouraged. This can be hard to do, but if you look at it with a big-picture and long-term view, it gets much easier. Also, I learned early on not to take NO personally. It is very rare that someone is saying no because of you. It does happen but is very rare. I just look at their NO as meaning it isn't the right fit for them at that point in time, and that makes it much easier. The third important piece of advice I received was that it takes a lot of hard work and dedication to turn this into a full-time business. Therefore, I had to be willing to go through the frustrations and ups and downs of any business and continue until I became successful.

Why do you believe everyone should consider MLM as a multiple source of income?

I don't believe everyone should consider MLM as a multiple source of income, because it is not a great fit for all personalities. I know being an accountant wouldn't fit my personality, but it does work for others. That being said, anyone who is willing and likes to talk with people should definitely consider it as a possible option and a way to diversify their income and not just rely on their job or current business.

It Doesn't Matter Where You Start
By Mari Santo-Domingo, PUERTO RICO

Have you ever felt that everything around you is not working to your advantage? Have you ever questioned why you are where you are today? Have you ever wondered if you have been the author of your own downfall?

My entire life fit into two suitcases, and while I waited for a taxi at the airport in Puerto Rico, I thought, *Okay, Mari. Here you are, back home, with nothing. What are you going to do now? Where are you going to start?* Sighing heavily as I looked up at the blue sky, the sun beating down on me, I checked my watch and took stock of just how I had come to be here.

I grew up in a small town on the island of Puerto Rico, and it is very interesting how you think and behave when you are an islander. You think you are the center of the world, and sometimes you might behave like it. It is not until you leave the island that you will realize the world is as big as your reality. I had left the island in 1985 looking for a change, better opportunities, a better lifestyle—the American dream!

I was a competitive workaholic; I had no boundaries and loved challenges. I had many doors closed in my face, but I always repeated to myself the advice my grandfather had shared with me: "Mari, if you know how to knock on doors, if you know how to be visible, what seems impossible will show up; it doesn't matter where you start or where you come from."

I'd started an image consulting business with a friend in Miami, and we were doing great, on our way to becoming a huge success—until one day, she told me she would have to bow out. As it stood, I couldn't afford the office costs on my own, and shortly after my partner left, I was forced to close the business for good.

With the business gone, I had no source of income. I started searching for A JOB; meanwhile I had to resort to living off my credit cards. In those days, I didn't know any better—to me, a wallet full of credit cards and store cards for every single establishment was like a status tag. It meant that I was good, that I was doing well, and that I was *better*. There are consequences to every decision: I knew that then, but what other option did I have?

Within three months, I had lost everything. Not only my business and my perfect credit score, but also my confidence and self-worth. Luckily, I had a friend with an apartment she wasn't using who kindly offered to let me use it. I walked into her 600 square-foot efficiency studio in two minds: on one hand, I was grateful not to be completely homeless, to have a roof over my head and a bed to sleep in. On the other, I was in financial ruin and had no idea how to go about piecing the tatters of my life back together.

I was blessed to have people around me that cared, and one friend in particular made a point of calling me almost every day to check in and see how I was doing. She took me by the hand and allowed me to be in a space where I wasn't thinking to myself, *Mari, you're alone.* It was another friend who introduced me to the MLM industry, an industry that gave me the tools and proven systems to build a home-based business. It was also this friend who finally told me that I had to face the facts of my situation as it stood right at that moment.

When she found out that I only had enough money for pizza, corn flakes, and Coca-Cola, she looked me right in the eye and said, "Mari, you have to go back home."

I had always been so sure, so completely certain that I would not go back to my parents in Puerto Rico, but at that point there really was no other option left for me. Of course, it wasn't like I could just pluck the money for a plane ticket out of thin air, and knowing that my parents were going through some big financial hardship of their own at the time, I was resolutely against asking them for the money. Thankfully, a friend from college loaned me the money.

During my first couple of weeks back, I took the time to consider what it was that I truly wanted out of life. In all of the jobs I'd had since leaving home, I'd started out at the bottom and worked my way to the top. When in big need, the world doesn't need to know—applying for a "cameo" role in the movie of your life is not going to kill you but staying "cameo" will. In my first job I applied to be a receptionist, and six months later I was sales manager. I learned that working at the front desk, you will know everybody and have the opportunity to study all departments and make the right connections to move ahead.

Even with this level of success, there had always seemed to be something missing, something that would never quite "click." It was being around my parents again, who were entrepreneurs and had had their own business for 25 years at this point, that helped slot into place the last piece of the puzzle. When I realized it, I laughed out loud—it should have been so obvious! I'd always wanted to be well-known, admired, and remembered—I wasn't ever someone who was happy to settle for mediocrity—but I'd never been able to decide on a career path.

I realized I was meant to be an entrepreneur, not an employee. The MLM industry allows you to have your own worldwide business.

This was the loudest wake-up call. I needed a major attitude adjustment: I was back to square one, completely starting over from zero, and I had to become an observer of the uncomfortable situation I was facing in order to see everything clearly. I had to step back and say, "I don't want to be at the mercy of anyone or anything ever again."

There's nothing like a bad experience to put you off a particular course of action, but the option you refuse to consider based on a past experience may often be the most profitable one to take. Saying, "I won't do that again," or, "I won't go back home," just because things didn't work like you expected simply skews your vision and renders you less able to recognize an opportunity when it occurs. I'd had it all and lost it all—now, I had to completely overhaul myself: I had to develop my character, drop pettiness and my reliance on the image I had of myself, train my mind, and listen to and enjoy my life.

The MLM industry suddenly looked like the beacon lighting my way. It allowed me to be exposed to coaches, trainers, and mentors—people that had done it before and could show me the path. But first, I realized, I had to start knocking on those doors again. I had to learn everything I could from the people I earned access to by being visible, and take it all in, so that I didn't have to reinvent the wheel.

It took discipline to conquer the nagging voices in my mind: I was too critical, always thinking that everything had to be perfect, but I learned to embrace my imperfections. Les Brown once said, "Just because you don't see it, it doesn't mean it's not coming," and

I finally understood, some problems are not going to be solved—they will only be outlived. In order to outlive the problems, I at least had to be present and visible for them and learn from each experience.

Action must follow learning, and after my setback and experiences in Miami, I took everything I had learned from my mentors and coaches and put it to work. I settled back home, got married to my soul mate, Miguel—who has also been my business partner of 27 years—and together we built a multimillion-dollar home-based business, broke company sales and recruiting records, and also helped several companies launch their line of products, programs and/or systems into the Hispanic market not only in the island but on the mainland, too.

Everything will start not only with you, but with your capacity of showing up and being visible in your leadership. A home-based business may not be for everybody, but *anybody* can learn the skills and disciplines to grow one that is sustainable and profitable. You have to stand out, be different, noteworthy, and unforgettable—these are qualities you need in order to not only knock on all the doors you can, but to keep those doors from being closed on you.

When I was focused on what I needed, what I didn't have, what I was missing, everything stopped. But the minute I started thinking and strategizing on how to bless others, help and serve them, build and empower them, the phone started ringing. Referrals, prospects, new programs, new opportunities, new proposals and deals were on the doorstep.

You will never know what is on the other side of the door, but instead of being scared of it, embrace the unknown. Take risks and don't be afraid of failure—your eagerness to take on uncertainty, backed by thorough preparation, will motivate you and those around you to help you rise above and become visible in life and leadership. The question shouldn't be, "When do I stop knocking on doors?" The question should be, "What if the next door is the one?"

George Eliot once said, "It is never too late to be what you might have been." Today I let inspiration come from the connection to the most powerful light that emanates from my heart's radiance where the Creator seeded our divine purpose. Now, living in my purpose and doing what I was meant to do, I realize more strongly than ever that it doesn't matter *when* or *where* you start. Just that you start at all.

Recommended Reading

As a Man Thinketh, by James Allen (originally written in the late 1800s, published in 1902)

Ben & Jerry's: The Inside Scoop, by Fred "Chico" Lager (Crown, 1994)

Beyond the Norm, by Norm Miller and H. K. Hosier (Thomas Nelson, 1996)

Harry and Ike, by Steve Neal (Simon & Schuster, 2002)

How to Fire Your Boss and Hire Yourself, by Foster Owusu (Kudo Communications, 2014)

Made in America, by Sam Walton and John Huey (Bantam Books, 1993)

Pampered Chef (The), by Doris Christopher (Currency Doubleday, 2005)

Snowball (The), by Alice Schroeder (Bantam Books, 2008)

Starbucks Experience (The), by Joseph Michelli (McGraw-Hill, 2007)

Time to Make the Donuts, by William Rosenberg (Lebhar-Friedman, 2001)

Where Have All the Leaders Gone?, by Lee Iacocca (Scribner, 2007)

Books Published by Tremendous Leadership
(www.TremendousLeadership.com)

A Message to Millennials, by Tracey C Jones

Being Tremendous: The Life, Lessons, and Legacy of Charlie "Tremendous" Jones

Beyond Tremendous, by Tracey C Jones
Life Is Tremendous, by Charlie "Tremendous" Jones
Moving Up—2020 and Beyond, by John Solleder
Poor, Smart, Rich: Moving from Poverty to Middle Class and Beyond, by John Segal
Sales Messenger (The): 10 Lessons for Success in Your Business and Personal Life, by Mary Anne Wihbey Davis
Saucy Aussie Living, by Tracey C Jones
Secret of Success (The), by R. C. Allen
Setting a True Course: Flight Plans for Life, by Gerry Wevodau
SPARK: 5 Essentials to Ignite the Greatness Within, by Dr. Tracey C Jones
True Blue Leadership, by Tracey C Jones

Short, impactful reads from the Life-Changing Classics Series

3 Therapies of Life (The), by Charlie "Tremendous" Jones; foreword by Dr. Tracey C. Jones
7 Golden Rules of Milton Hershey (The), by Greg Rothman; foreword by Richard Zimmerman
7 Leadership Virtues of Joan of Arc (The), by Peter Darcy
Acres of Diamonds, by Russell H. Conwell; appreciation by John Wanamaker
Advantages of Poverty, by Andrew Carnegie; foreword by Dale Carnegie
As a Man Thinketh, by James Allen
Books Are Tremendous, edited by Charlie "T" Jones; introduction by J. C. Penney
Bradford, You're Fired!, by William W. Woodbridge
Breakthrough Speaking, by Mark Sanborn
Character Building, by Booker T. Washington
Discipleship, by John M. Segal
From Belfast to Narnia: The Life and Faith of C. S. Lewis, by The C. S. Lewis Institute
Greatest Thing in the World (The), by Henry Drummond; introduction by Dwight L. Moody
Key to Excellence (The), by Charlie "T" Jones

Recommended Reading

Kingship of Self-Control (The), by William George Jordan; foreword by Charlie "T" Jones

Lincoln Ideals (The), edited by Charlie "T" Jones

Luther on Leadership, by Stephen J. Nichols

Maxims of Life & Business, by John Wanamaker; foreword by Elbert Hubbard and Russell Conwell

Message to Garcia (A), by Elbert Hubbard

My Conversion, by Charles Spurgeon; edited and compiled by Charlie "T" Jones

Mystery of Self-Motivation (The), by Charlie "T" Jones

New Common Denominator of Success (The), by Albert E. N. Gray; foreword by Charlie "T" Jones

Price of Leadership (The), by Charlie "T" Jones; foreword by Dr. Tracey C. Jones

Reason Why (The), by R. A. Laidlaw; introduction by Marjorie Blanchard

Ronald Wilson Reagan: The Great Communicator, by Greg Rothman

Science of Getting Rich: Abridged Edition (The), by Wallace D. Wattles; edited by Charlie "T" Jones

Self-Improvement through Public Speaking, by Orison Swett Marden; introduction by Forrest Wallace Cato

Succeeding with What You Have, by Charles Schwab; foreword by Andrew Carnegie

That Something, by William W. Woodbridge; introduction by Paul J. Meyer

Three Decisions (The), by Charlie "T" Jones; foreword by Dr. Tracey C. Jones

Walt Disney: Dreams Really Do Come True!, by Jason Liller

Wit and Wisdom of General George S. Patton (The), compiled by Charlie "T" Jones

www.ingramcontent.com/pod-product-compliance
Lightning Source LLC
Chambersburg PA
CBHW070638050426
42451CB00008B/212